D1556907

The Fabulous
Vaughan Brothers

The Fabulous Vaughan Brothers

Jimmie and Stevie Ray

James L. Dickerson

TAYLOR TRADE PUBLISHING
Lanham • New York • Dallas • Boulder • Toronto • Oxford

Published by Taylor Trade Publishing
An imprint of The Rowman & Littlefield Publishing Group, Inc.
4501 Forbes Boulevard, Suite 200
Lanham, Maryland 20706

Distributed by National Book Network

Library of Congress Cataloging-in-Publication Data

Dickerson, James L.
  The fabulous Vaughan brothers : Jimmie and Stevie Ray / James L. Dickerson.—
1st Taylor Trade pub. ed.
      p. cm.
  Includes bibliographical references (p.   ), discography and index.
  ISBN 1-58979-116-9 (hardcover : alk. paper)
  1. Vaughan brothers. 2. Blues musicians—United States—Biography.
3. Rock musicians—United States—Biography. I. Title.
ML421.V38D43 2004
781.66'092'2—dc22   2003024505

⊗™ The paper used in this publication meets the minimum requirements of American National Standard for Information Sciences—Permanence of Paper for Printed Library Materials, ANSI/NISO Z39.48–1992.
Manufactured in the United States of America.

Contents

To Brown Burnett

Who writes the blues, sings the blues, talks the blues

Foreword

WRITING THIS BOOK was an eighteen-year project. There have been two biographies written about Stevie Ray Vaughan, Keri Leigh's *Stevie Ray: Soul to Soul*, and Joe Nick Patoski's and Bill Crawford's *Stevie Ray Vaughan: Caught in the Crossfire*. But I wanted to write a book that gave equal attention to Jimmie's band, the Fabulous Thunderbirds—and to his subsequent solo career—and to the brothers' recording experiences in Memphis, which I see as more important to their overall development as recording artists than their experiences in Texas.

I first met Jimmie and Stevie Ray Vaughan in 1985 while writing stories for my Memphis-based magazine, *Nine-O-One Network*. Over the next five years, up until Stevie's death, I interviewed and photographed Jimmie's band, the Fabulous Thunderbirds, and Stevie and his band, Double Trouble, numerous times, and had them as guests on my hour-long, internationally syndicated radio program, *Pulsebeat—Voice of the Heartland*, which I produced in association with KFFA in Helena, Arkansas.

When I used quotations in this book that came from my own interviews, I did not attribute them as such because it would have been too awkward to continuously refer to statements as so-and-so told "me." Readers may assume that all unattributed quotations in this book were drawn from interviews conducted by the author.

I would like to thank the following people and institutions for their help with this book: the late Stevie Ray Vaughan, who was always a pleasure to be around; Jimmie Vaughan, not so much for his recent cooperation (he has become somewhat disagreeable in his old age), but for his openness and good cheer while he was making the music; Kim Wilson, for always finding the time to talk about what he loved the most—his music; B. B. King, a true gentleman who, over a period of many years, has never failed to make time for music talk; Robert Cray, Preston Hubbard, Fran Christina, Brown Burnett, John Hampton, Jim Gaines, John Fry; the staff at the Memphis and Shelby County Library; Don Nix, Bobby "Blue" Bland, Ron Wood, the late Carl Perkins, Chips Moman, Jerry Lee Lewis, Bobby Manuel, Carla Thomas, Bobby Womack, Estelle Axton; Klaudia Kroboth for sending original music during the writing of the book; the staff at PhotoFest for helping me round out my photo package; the staff at the Public Library of Nashville and Davidson County; the staff at the Jean and Alexander Heard Library at Vanderbilt University; the staff at the Eudora Welty Library in Jackson, Mississippi; Michael Dorr, and Ross Plotkin at Cooper Square Press.

CHAPTER 1

Jimmie and Stevie Ray: Viva la Revolution!

I N THE EARLY 1950s, Texas was a seething cauldron of gritty, pulsating musical influences. The state's growing African American population imported the blues from the Mississippi Delta. Hispanics brought in Spanish influences from Mexico and beyond, especially as it applied to the guitar— Spain's contribution to the music of the world. And poor whites had latched onto the catchy country and folk melodies that trickled in during the nation's westward expansion.

In those days, there were two kinds of music in Texas: American music—popular radio music recorded by the likes of Tony Bennett, Patti Page, Eddie Fisher, and Doris Day—and homegrown Texas music, which was exemplified by Bob Wills and the Texas Playboys, Bobby "Blue" Bland, who was born in Tennessee but recorded and performed in Texas, Clarence "Gatemouth" Brown, T-Bone Walker, Lightnin' Hopkins, and Hank Thompson and his Brazos Valley Boys.

So-called American music was directed at the middle and upper classes, the people who had thirty-year mortgages, white-collar jobs, and college-bound children. Texas music was more of an underground phenomenon aimed at the working class, those who wore

1

white socks and brown shoes, and were derogatorily called *niggers, spics,* and *rednecks*, the people who spilled their sweat and blood to build and service the clanking machinery of the American Dream.

It was into that world that Jimmie "Big Jim" Vaughan entered by way of Rockwall, Texas, where he was born the son of a sharecropper. His father died when he was seven, leaving him, his mother, and his seven siblings to fend for themselves. It was a rough introduction to life. Statistics tell us that sons without fathers are more likely to spend time in jail, see violence as a problem-solving tool, drop out of school, and become alcoholics and addicts than their more family-friendly counterpoints. Big Jim was dealt a bad hand from the get-go.

Not surprisingly, he dropped out of school when he was sixteen and enlisted in the navy. America was in the midst of World War II and Big Jim was sent to the South Pacific, where he grew up in a man's world far removed from the one that he had known with his mother. After the war, he returned to Texas and settled in Oak Cliff, a suburb of Dallas, where he found work as a sales clerk at a 7-Eleven convenience store.

One of Big Jim's favorite customers was Martha Jean Cook, a graduate of Sunset High School. Unlike Big Jim, she grew up in an intact family that was somewhat more prosperous than his, one that had experienced few serious bumps along life's highway. Her father, who worked as a foreman at the Lone Star Gas Company, was often described as easygoing. For Martha, the world was a beautiful place, filled with great promise.

In the late 1940s, 7-Eleven described itself as a "convenience" store in a comprehensive sense of the word. When shoppers pulled up outside the store, they could honk their car horn and wait for an energetic young man wearing a white starched shirt and bland necktie to rush out to take their order.

Martha's order, which she placed on her way home from work as a secretary at a lumber company, was always the same—one Eskimo Pie, a frozen ice-cream confection that would melt on the spot if you didn't eat it quickly. The way they told it in later years, it was pretty much love at first sight. For Martha, the attraction lay in his earnest but polite manner as he took her order and his physical appearance, especially his large, well-shaped biceps. For Big Jim, it was her pretty face, her friendly personality—and the fact that she owned her own car.

Big Jim and Martha flirted their way through several Eskimo Pies before he got up enough nerve to ask her out on a date. Their personalities were very different—he was boisterous and quick-tempered, prone to drink too much, and she was quiet and emotionally pliable, the stereotypical southern lady—but that initial attraction quickly turned into love. After a short courtship, they were married on January 13, 1950.

What Big Jim and Martha most had in common was a love of music. They didn't play musical instruments, but they loved to dance and they went to juke joints and ballrooms at every opportunity. Music was the bond that cemented their romance. Actually, you might say that music ran in both their families. Big Jim had relatives who played in bands with Glenn Miller and Tommy Dorsey, and Martha had relatives who played in country swing bands in the Dallas area.

With marriage came new responsibilities for Big Jim. Because he couldn't support his new wife on a 7-Eleven carhop salary, he gained membership in the local asbestos workers union (with the help of one of his brothers) and quickly found work troweling the fibrous mineral around pipes and air ducts in office buildings, refineries, and power plants. At that time, asbestos was considered a scientific marvel and nothing was known of its deadly cancer-causing potential; Big Jim thought he was on the cutting edge of American industrial progress.

On March 20, 1951, a little over fourteen months after Big Jim and Martha said their marriage vows, she gave birth at Baylor Medical Center to a son, Jimmie Lawrence Vaughan, named after his father and the physician who delivered him. He weighed five pounds and was seventeen and one-half inches long.

Big Jim and Martha took Jimmie home with them from the hospital, convinced that life couldn't possibly get any better. Big Jim had a good job and Martha had the family she always wanted. They settled into a routine that was characterized by the popular movies of the day—*Death of a Salesman*, *The African Queen*, and *High Noon*—and the mellow music of the late Glenn Miller.

Three and a half years later, Martha gave birth at Methodist Hospital to their second son. He was the same length as his brother, but he weighed only three pounds, nine and one-quarter ounces—a surprise since he arrived two weeks late. Because of his low birth weight, he was kept in the hospital for three weeks for observation. Perhaps because they were expecting a girl this time, Big Jim and Martha did not decide on a name until they actually filled out the birth certificate. With no one special in mind, they named him Stephan Ray Vaughan, a name they chose because they thought it had a nice ring to it.

For the first few years, the Vaughan brothers' life was filled with uncertainty. When work was unavailable in Dallas, Big Jim followed construction sites across the South, taking his family with him to Louisiana, Mississippi, and Arkansas, and then back to Texas again when the work was there. Sometimes they only lived in a town for several weeks; other times it stretched out to several months. The brothers never had time to make friends or develop a sense of place.

"Well, it wasn't really a comfortable *Leave It to Beaver* kind of a deal, you know?" Jimmie later explained to VH1 *Legends*. "Moving all the time and never really getting to know people, on the highway all the time and going to school for two weeks here and three weeks there. It was the absolute perfect training for us to do what we did."

Eventually Big Jim found enough work in and around Dallas to buy his family a modest home in the Oak Cliff section of town. That brought an end to the brothers' peripatetic lifestyle, but it unleashed a different sort of uncertainty. Being out on the road all the time, going from place to place, had dissipated a lot of Big Jim's pent-up frustrations, lending an air of legitimacy to his dark, son-without-a-father vision of life. Now that he was basically working nine to five, returning home at the end of each day to his family, he drank to relieve his tensions and, according to some accounts, took his frustrations out on his family.

"My father was an alcoholic, and his dad was an alcoholic as well," Stevie explained later in life. "That's something I've come to grips with. He didn't like the way he felt or the way he treated us, but it was the only way he knew. There were some hard times at home, a lot of fighting."

Jimmie, perhaps because he was the older brother, learned how to roll with the emotional punches delivered by his father and he accepted them at face value, but Stevie did not adjust quite as well. He spent much of his childhood fearing the unknown, afraid to be left alone. He was sickly as a young child, plagued with frequent sinus problems. When he was five, he underwent surgery to correct the problem; the operation was successful, but it left him with a somewhat flattened nose, setting him apart in appearance from Jimmie and the other children his own age.

The following year, when he was six, Stevie got into Big Jim's liquor cabinet and made himself a drink, he confessed to reporters in later years—and he was a serious drinker from that age on, his childhood dulled by the warm glow of a whisky buzz.

During Stevie's formative years something dreadful happened to him, something that he would very nearly take to his grave. Whether it had anything to do with his father or other family members is known only to a few confidants, but whatever its source, it had a profound impact on his later life.

Between the time Jimmie and Stevie were born and entered school, both the music scene and the social landscape of Texas changed radically. Born into racial segregation and the nuclear arms race with the Soviet Union, the two passionate issues of that era, they witnessed President Dwight Eisenhower send federal troops into Little Rock, Arkansas, in 1957 to desegregate the public schools in the South and they lived through the Cuban missile crisis in which President John F. Kennedy stared down the Soviet Union in the most dangerous confrontation of the nuclear age, only to be assassinated little more than a year later while visiting Dallas.

Those events had a profound effect on the Texas music scene. White, African American, and Hispanic musicians had associated with one another for decades, but never publicly, for that would have ended their careers and served as an invitation to violence.

The desegregation of schools and public facilities pulled back the curtain on those associations and, for the first time, made it acceptable for musicians of different races to perform in public together. That, coupled with the uncertainty associated with the nuclear arms race and the assassination of a president, had a freeing effect on musicians all across the state, as living for the moment became imminently more attractive to an artistic community that already lived hand to mouth.

The music revolution that transformed Texas began in January 1955, when the Blue Moon Boys (Elvis Presley, Scotty Moore, and Bill Black) crossed through Arkansas for their first tour of the Lone Star state. Rock 'n' roll spread from town to town like wildfire, inspiring Texans, most notably Buddy Holly and the Crickets, to develop their own style of music.

By 1955 Holly had cut several demo recordings. The music coming out of Memphis set his soul on fire and he was convinced that he could be a player in what was viewed at ground zero as a true revolution in music. Unfortunately Holly took a wrong turn on his way to Tennessee and ended up in Nashville instead of Memphis, a bad decision that sent him on what amounted to a wild-goose chase into the then-barren world of country music, before he discovered his rock 'n' roll legs and subsequently recorded hits such as "Peggy Sue" and "Oh, Boy!"

A parallel music explosion occurred in the black community as T-Bone Walker, Clarence "Gatemouth" Brown, Lightnin' Hopkins, and Johnny Hopkins transformed the blues with electric guitar licks that flirted with the rock 'n' roll sensibilities brought to Texas by the Blue Moon Boys. Stirring that mix was the Tennessee-born Bobby "Blue" Bland, who preferred the big band sound of saxophones and trumpets. With hits such as "Turn on Your Love Light," "Stormy Monday Blues," and "Cry, Cry, Cry," all wildly popular on college campuses across the South, he did as much as anyone to break down racial barriers in music.

Jimmie was the first member of the Vaughan family to sign up for the new music revolution. It happened by accident. In 1964, at the age of thirteen, Jimmie was more interested in football than music, but an accident on the playing field left him with a broken collarbone and laid him up for a time, dampening his enthusiasm for the sport. While he was recuperating from his injury, a friend of Big Jim's dropped off a battered old guitar that was missing three strings for

Jimmie. The friend advised Jimmie to play music instead of football since he couldn't get hurt doing that.

Jimmie took to the guitar right away, teaching himself to make music with the three existing strings. Several days later, when the friend stopped by to visit Big Jim, Jimmie showed him several songs he had composed. The friend was so impressed that he took the guitar back long enough to have it restrung and then re-presented it to Jimmie with a suggestion that he give it his best shot.

At that time, the Beatles were dominating the airwaves with hits such as "I Want to Hold Your Hand," "Hard Day's Night" and "Eight Days a Week," the Kingsmen with "Louie, Louie," and the Animals with "House of the Rising Sun," but Dallas radio stations such as KNOX and XERB, which featured the legendary Wolfman Jack, also provided their audiences with a steady diet of classic rock and rhythm and blues.

When the time came to work up his first real song, Jimmie looked to the past for a gritty song with a distinct guitar part that he had heard on the radio with his father—Bill Doggett's 1956 hit, "Honky Tonk." Next came a song recorded by a local band named the Nightcaps, a take on Lil' Son Jackson's "Drinkin' Wine Spo-Dee-O-Dee."

All that musical activity did not go unnoticed by brother Stevie, who had acquired musical aspirations of his own at the age of ten. He wanted to be like his big brother, but not *too much* like him, so he tried different instruments. Martha and Big Jim gave him a toy Sears & Roebuck guitar with cowboys on it, but he was more interested in the drums. He fashioned a homemade set out of shoeboxes and tried his hand at that, but lost interest after his parents asked him to stop making so much noise. Next he tried a saxophone and—because all he could squeeze out of the instrument were a few irritating, high-pitched squeaks—he put it aside before he was ordered to do so.

While all eyes were on Jimmie, Stevie quietly returned to his guitar, encouraged more by his brother than by his parents, but even that had limits. "When he started really trying to play, I would put [my guitar] down and leave and say, 'Look, don't touch my guitar or I'm gonna, you know, I'm gonna really get mad,'" Jimmie told

VH1 *Legends*. "And I would leave, and he would play the guitar just as soon as I left."

Once asked if they swapped ideas during that time, Stevie laughed and said, "Well, it was pretty much him having the ideas and me trying to figure out what they were. After several years, I started getting used to learning by myself. First he taught me a lot about playing and then he taught me to teach myself, which was a great thing."

As Stevie learned the basics, Jimmie got serious about playing in a band of his own. That meant learning enough songs to perform for two or three hours. To do that, Jimmie scoured local record stores, searching for music that he felt would be appropriate for a teen band. He gravitated not to the popular music of the day—the Beatles, Gerry and the Pacemakers, Herman's Hermits, or even Elvis Presley—but rather to the roots music that fueled the underground movement then taking place across the South.

The heroes of that movement were Jimmy Reed, Muddy Waters, Freddie King, B. B. King, and Bobby "Blue" Bland, African Americans who were unaffected by the British invasion of the pop charts. "Jimmie would bring home, when he was fifteen, everyone from Kenny Burrell to Jimmy Reed to Albert King to B. B. King, Buddy Guy, and Muddy Waters," recalled Stevie. "He was bringing home records that a fifteen-year-old was not supposed to be getting a hold of. And he was also getting a hold of a lot of the more popular players like Hendrix and the Blues Breakers and things like that at the same time. Through him, I had an influence of the blues masters, jazz people, and a lot of the updated rehashes. We got to hear the original blues masters and people doing this in a new wave at the same time. So I got a more free-spirited look at it early on in the early to mid-1960s. I was only about ten years old. That was quite a shot in the arm."

In 1966, when Jimmie was fifteen, he dropped out of high school and joined his first band, a group named the Penetrations. It featured Sammy Loria as the vocalist, with Jimmie on rhythm guitar and Johnny Peebles on lead guitar.

When they weren't performing, Jimmie sought out guitarist Freddie King, a six-foot-seven African American who performed regularly in Dallas's black nightclubs. The Texas-born singer, who had made a name for himself in Chicago, where he learned to play the music of Jimmie Rogers and Eddie Taylor, had recorded a number of national hits such as "Have You Ever Loved a Woman," the "Stumble," and "Hideaway," before moving to Dallas.

"I saw him [perform] more than anybody," Jimmie told Larry Birnbaum for *Down Beat* magazine. "I followed him around for years, and I even played rhythm with him for a little while. . . . I play more like Freddie King than anybody—I mean, it might not sound like Freddie, but it's the same."

For Stevie, Jimmie's musical discoveries were mind-boggling. "It was like Martian stuff," he said of the Muddy Waters, B. B. King, and Beatles records that Jimmie brought home with him. "I had never heard anything like it before. Then there was this Jimi Hendrix record that he found. There was this show called *Something Else,* a popular music show, and it was one of the records they didn't go for and they threw it in the trash and Jimmie happened to see a little paragraph in a music magazine about him and he brought the record home.

"With hearing people like Muddy Waters at the same time, it was easy to see the connection between the two types of music. It was a real exciting thing. And it made a lot of connection up here [tapping his head] and in my heart as well about what to do with all these different influences."

Big Jim generally supported his sons' musical ambitions, but there were limits to what he would tolerate. "There were times when [having two guitarists in the home] was a real good thing and there were times when that was not what he wanted," Stevie recalled. "Teenagers in the 1960s were apt to turn things up real loud and that can get old when you just come home from work, but my parents have been very supportive of what Jimmie and I have done, pretty much the whole time."

Although Jimmie and Stevie shared a common interest in music, Jimmie never saw his younger brother as a real competitor. On the contrary, he saw Stevie more as a fan, someone who hung on his every word. It never entered his mind then that Stevie would ever be as talented as he was on the guitar.

All that changed when Jimmie joined a new band called the Chessmen. Doyle Bramhall, the singer, was visiting Jimmie one day when he heard music coming from another part of the house. He knew it wasn't Jimmie because had just walked past him. He investigated and found Stevie sitting on the floor of his room with a hollow-body Gibson Messenger that his brother had given him, playing a Jeff Beck song titled "Jeff's Boogie." He was astonished at Stevie's level of playing, as was Jimmie, who had not been paying much attention to his younger brother's exploding guitar skills. On that day the brothers developed a true sibling rivalry, with each brother determined to outdo the other.

The Chessman played only cover songs but landed bookings all over Texas. One of the most important bookings they ever got was as an opening act for Jimi Hendrix at a Houston venue and at Dallas's McFarlin Auditorium. To Stevie's delight, Jimmie obtained Hendrix's autograph for him. It was a treasure that Stevie carried in his wallet until the ink faded and the paper rotted away to nothing.

Stevie and Big Jim and Martha hated to see Jimmie drop out of school—lord knows, that decision was preceded by terrible family fights. But he showed no inclination for academics and felt so passionate about his music that there was no way they could force him to attend classes that he felt were irrelevant. Because he was still living at home, they felt they could exert some measure of control over his life.

All that changed when the Chessmen fell apart, primarily because Doyle contracted hepatitis and was laid up for a couple of months. When he was feeling better, he and Jimmie formed a new band they named Texas Storm. Filled with hopes and dreams of stardom, Jimmie ran away from home with the band and went to Los Angeles, where they felt they could break into the big time.

"I thought you could just practice your guitar and then all of a sudden you had a hit record," Jimmie later explained to Larry Birnbaum for a story in *Guitar World*. "I didn't realize that there was anything else involved."

After three miserable months in Los Angeles, Jimmie returned to Dallas, his hopes for stardom dashed. He married his girlfriend Donna and she quickly became pregnant with a girl they named Tina. To support his family, Jimmie put his guitar away for a while and worked at a series of day jobs—most notably as a garbage man for the Irving sanitation department—but he quickly saw that was going to be a dead end, so he picked up his guitar again and looked for a new band.

Not finding what he was looking for in Dallas, Jimmie moved to Austin, where the music scene was beginning to attract national attention.

With Jimmie gone, Stevie stepped up his own efforts, but without the unqualified support that Big Jim and Martha had afforded Jimmie in the beginning of his career. "When he left they felt as if they had lost Jimmie and that they were going to lose me, too," said Stevie. "There was a period where we didn't hear from Jimmie for a long time. It's just that he was on the road playing rock 'n' roll and trying to learn it—life—that way and that's the hard way."

Stevie joined his first band, Blackbird, when he was fourteen, playing after school and on weekends. By then he had acquired a second guitar from Jimmie, a 1952 Fender Broadcaster. Mostly the band played for free—when they could talk someone into listening. Stevie purchased his first record around that time, a copy of Lonnie Mack's instrumental hit, "Wham." Prior to that he had no need to buy records of his own because Jimmie had kept him supplied. Stevie tore "Wham" down, note by note, until he knew it by heart. "Wham" represented a major difference between the brothers: as a guitarist, Jimmie was into the feel of the music, without much regard for the more technical aspects. Stevie was just the opposite. He cared greatly about the technical characteristics of the music and expressed his feel for the music in that way.

Unfortunately Big Jim didn't have the same appreciation for "Wham" that Stevie did. He played it so often that one day his father snatched the record off the turntable and broke it into pieces. Undeterred, Stevie went out and purchased another copy. This time he borrowed a friend's PA system, placed microphones in front of the speakers, and cranked it up as loud as it would go. Big Jim broke the record as soon as he heard it—and so it went, with father and son both retreating to their rooms to get drunk, growing further apart with each new escalation.

At age twelve, Stevie got an after-school job as a restaurant dishwasher. "One of my jobs was to clean out this trash bin next to a grease vat. Well, I was standing on the cover of that thing and it caved in. I fell in it and someone almost poured hot grease all over me by accident—I could have been killed," said Stevie. "Well, I told the woman I was working for about it and she just started telling me about how much it was gonna cost me to pay for that lid. She wouldn't even let me use the office phone. I walked through the restaurant to the pay phone, twelve years old, covered with grease, called my mom to come get me and told her the whole story so everybody in the restaurant could hear it. People started leaving—it was great!"

His stint at the restaurant was Stevie's first—and only—day job. He decided right then and there that he was going to play guitar for a living. Jimmie had proved to him that playing music for a living was an attainable goal.

As Stevie began to get in touch with his own sensibilities as a musician, he drifted away from his mother and father. In the beginning, when Jimmie first started playing the guitar, Big Jim and Martha were proud of him and often showed him off to their friends. When Stevie followed in his footsteps, they thought it was cute the way he idolized his big brother.

As Jimmie's forays into the Dallas music scene began to involve late hours, alcohol and drugs, and wild girls that Big Jim and Martha considered on the unsavory side, they saw guitar playing in an entirely different light. Music became their enemy, the satanic pied piper of the youth culture that was turning America inside out with its new vision of where society was headed.

Big Jim had some terrific fights with Jimmie over his rejection of values that Jim held dear. Similar fights took place all across the country among parents and their sons and daughters, as the Woodstock generation took to the streets to protest the Vietnam War, government corruption, corporate greed, and institutional racism.

When Jimmie left home to play in a rock 'n' roll band, he left behind unresolved issues that Big Jim was incapable of moving past. That put Stevie in the wrong place at the wrong time. He was not as outgoing as his big brother, so his rebellion was not as noticeable to his parents, but he felt the same way Jimmie did and he knew it was only a matter of time before he would be found out.

To placate his parents, Stevie enrolled in night classes at Southern Methodist University, an experimental arts program that was open to high-school students. The idea was for the students to express their creativity in any way they chose. They could paint a great work of art, or they could shape a sculpture into anything they wished and then smash it to bits with a hammer, all in the name of self-expression. That doesn't make much sense, but it was, after all, the late 1960s, a time of self-indulgent extremes.

Stevie used the class as an opportunity to talk about the records he loved, hardly what Big Jim and Martha had in mind. They figured he was getting an education, something that would take him away from rock 'n' roll, but, to his way of thinking, it only gave the music he loved more credibility. After completing the course, Stevie revved up his musical ambitions again, prompting more outbursts from Big Jim about his music and dire warnings from him that he should stop dressing like black people.

CHAPTER 2

Fabulous Thunderbirds
Break Out of the Pack

T HE PROBLEM with Dallas was that it had no soul, at least that was the way Jimmie saw it. Nightclub owners would not book bands that did original songs or played any type of roots music, especially blues. All they wanted to hear in their clubs were Top 40 covers, the type of music that would bring in young couples with lots of money.

Austin was different. Perhaps because of its status as the state capital, or perhaps because of a strong liberal arts focus at the University of Texas (two factors that attracted dreamers, hippies, and would-be Sam Houstons from all across the state), Austin nightclubs were open to just about anything.

If it is possible for a city to have a mentality, Austin's is a willingness to try just about anything once or twice. Located 200 miles south of Dallas, 80 miles northeast of San Antonio, and 225 miles from the Mexican border, it is far enough away from Middle America to feel culturally isolated and close enough to Mexico to have a sense of decadent internationalism.

Musically, Austin was a mixture of blues and country, with rock 'n' roll nipping at the traditions of each. In the early 1970s, Fort

Worth native Willie Nelson settled in Austin after failing to find success as a country artist in Nashville, where he landed a spot on the *Grand Ole Opry* but never made hit records of his own, despite penning major hits for artists as diverse as Stevie Wonder, Roy Orbison, Frank Sinatra, Perry Como, and Aretha Franklin.

Nelson had a hunch about his music. He felt there was an audience for what he was doing with the young, long-haired generation that shared his antiestablishment views about life. He asked the management of the most popular rock club in Austin, the Armadillo World Headquarters, to give him a chance. He was an immediate success and soon opened his own nightclub in Austin.

By 1975, Nelson had a Top 10 single, "Blue Eyes Cryin' in the Rain," which he followed up with a platinum album, *Red-Headed Stranger*, and *Wanted: The Outlaws*, an album he recorded with fellow Texan Waylon Jennings. In that eclectic Austin atmosphere, where every musician considered himself or herself a renegade of one sort or another, the outlaw movement in country music was spawned.

The same sort of thing was happening in Austin with blues and rock 'n' roll. The blues were touched up for the city's white audiences, and rock 'n' roll was dirtied down and spiked with Delta blues licks for the city's black audiences. There were dozens, maybe hundreds, of bands in Austin in the early- to mid-1970s. Most of them never thought of having a recording contract. They just wanted to play the music that they loved and earn enough money to pay the bills.

As Willie Nelson's reputation grew, the city attracted a growing number of successful recording artists such as Doug Sahm's Sir Douglas Quintet, which had had a worldwide hit in 1965 with "She's about a Mover," Janis Joplin, who sang with a country band in Austin before going to California to join Big Brother and the Holding Company, and Johnny Winter, the first successful white blues guitarist from Texas.

Winter, who was born in Beaumont, Texas, raised the bar for white guitarists in 1969 when he recorded his album, *Progressive Blues Experiment*, at Austin's most popular nightclub, Vulcan Gas Company. It was the sort of place that was despised and feared by the city's white-collar workers, but loved by blue-collar workers, hippies, college students, and musicians. It was the only venue in Austin that would hire twenty-five-year-old Winter and his band, made up of Uncle John Turner on drums and Tommy Shannon on bass. After they recorded the album, the band broke up. Winter went to England, where he thought audiences would be more receptive to his style of blues, and Shannon went to Dallas, where he hoped to get with another band.

On Shannon's first day back in Dallas, he dropped by a nightclub called the Fog to hook up with old friends. As he walked in the door, he was struck by the sounds of a guitar that stopped him dead in his tracks.

"There was this real awkward looking, scrawny, fourteen-year-old kid up there," Shannon later related to the *Dallas Observer*, telling of his first encounter with Stevie Ray Vaughan. "I knew then that he had something special. Back then he was like all kids. He was copying Eric Clapton and Jimi Hendrix and blues guys. He hadn't developed his own thing yet, but Stevie was so passionate. He loved it so deeply. He put on a guitar and something happened. It's like he went to a different state of consciousness. And you could see it and feel this pure source of energy go right through him."

For Jimmie, Austin looked like the Promised Land for more reasons than one. His marriage had fallen apart and he started dating a friend of Stevie's named Connie Crouch. Musically, Dallas seemed like a dead end. Jimmie was out of step with the Top 40 bands that were in demand and there were no recording or nightclub scenes to amount to anything. Starting over in a new town with a new woman seemed the thing to do.

Still hoping to make something of their band, Texas Storm, Jimmie and singer Doyle Bramhall packed up and moved to Austin, where they renamed the band simply Storm. Traveling with Jimmie was Connie Crouch, who quickly set up house for him in a rental unit in the working-class district of south Austin. Left behind were Jimmie's wife, Donna, and daughter, Tina. It was not a very admirable thing for Jimmie to do and it only confirmed Big Jim's and Martha's fears about his chosen career.

Jimmie and Bramhall both got day jobs as construction workers to support themselves while they performed at night with Storm.

Rather than perform music that he did not respect, Jimmie decided to play only the music that he loved, even if it meant working days on a construction site.

Jimmie quickly gained a reputation in Austin as the top up-and-coming guitarist on the scene. His good looks, his laid-back style of playing, his devotion to his music, all created an aura that was recognized by other musicians and by women who wanted to share intimate moments with him. For Becky Crabtree, it was love at first sight. Even though he was living with Connie and still recovering from his divorce, she made love to him, eventually becoming pregnant with a son she named Tyrone Vaughan.

Jimmie didn't take responsibility for the child, telling friends that he could not be certain that it was his, considering the way that everyone slept with everyone else in those days—and he put distance between himself and Crabtree, a decision that left her undeterred, for she readily told friends that Jimmie was the father of her child.

When Jimmie arrived in Austin, the Vulcan Gas Company was the center of musical activity, but within a year it was overshadowed by the Armadillo World Headquarters, a warehouse-turned-nightclub that blended national acts such as Frank Zappa and the Mothers of Invention with homegrown acts such as Willie Nelson, Leon Russell, and Freddie King. Jimmie's band Storm got its share of bookings there, but white blues bands never drew large enough crowds for band members to take home much money. The smaller clubs didn't pay as much, but they offered work on a regular basis, which was all that mattered to Jimmie and his band mates.

The first few years in Austin, Storm went through many changes. It was never a matter of getting the right mix of musicians to land a recording contract. Making records was the last thing on anyone's mind. It was simply about playing a good gig and everyone, including the band members, having a good time.

In 1972 a bass player named Keith Ferguson joined Storm for a short time. The twenty-five-year-old son of a concert pianist had made the rounds, including a stint with Johnny Winters, who never failed to dazzle him, both for his skill with a guitar and his combativeness. "We used to call him The Stork," Ferguson told the *Dallas Observer*. "Nobody messed with him. One night he knocked out an off-duty cop for calling him a girl. I saw Johnny Winters fight many times. He was real strong and mean. He'd go until you quit breathing and couldn't hurt him anymore."

Fighting was a way of life among band members in those days. Often the fights were over women. Other times it was due to the drugs and alcohol that were always overabundant. Sometimes it was simply out of the frustration of having million-dollar dreams while living in squalor. Whatever the reasons, it was rare for a band to play an entire night together without someone getting a little hot under the collar.

Sometimes Stevie went to Austin to hear Jimmie play. Friends remember him standing on chairs, hooting and hollering as big brother did his thing with a succession of faceless sidemen and singers. Everyone said that if Jimmie could sing he would be a star. He just had the right look, the right, bad-boy attitude to be convincing as a singer.

Occasionally Jimmie returned to Dallas to hear Stevie play. It thrilled Stevie to see his older brother in the audience, but more often than not, Jimmie told them they sucked. He thought Stevie tried too hard when he played and always seemed to be wrestling with his guitar, as if it were a wild animal that needed taming, instead of simply riding it with gentlemanly authority. Even so, Jimmie was impressed with the progress Stevie was making as a guitarist. There was never much doubt about why Stevie was working so hard: he wanted to beat big brother at his own game.

Music was all Stevie had at that point in his life. His parents' battles with Jimmie had carried over to him, making him the focus of their disappointment. They told him that he was wasting his time with music, that he was going to turn out bad just like Jimmie. Big Jim was not averse to making that point with a hard slap.

One day Stevie went to school with a bandage on his ear. When a classmate asked him what was wrong with his ear, Stevie told him that his father had struck him after an argument about his turning out just like Jimmie, a point of view that turned Stevie against his father not so much because of the slap, but because he had berated his brother and only hero in life.

Stevie was a failure at school because he had no interest in academic subjects. The more he tried to bolster his self-image by looking and dressing like a musician, the more disapproval he received from teachers and other students. By the time he entered his senior year at Kimball High School, he was embroiled in an ongoing battle over his hair with the principal, who had issued an order prohibiting all male students from wearing their hair past their collar or over their ears.

Stevie had his hair cut to specification but brushed it down over his face, since no mention was made of length in the front. This prompted dire threats from the principal. Although such grooming standards would be laughable by today's standards, the principal rightfully saw Stevie's behavior as a challenge to his authority. Before the principal could expel him, Stevie dropped out.

After several months of trying to keep the peace at home while struggling to keep Blackbird together, Stevie and the band packed up and moved to Austin, where they quickly became favorites with college audiences. Stevie lived like a vagabond, crashing with different friends, burdened with only his guitar and a portable record player.

Unlike Jimmie, Stevie liked the hippie subculture that dominated the college music scene. He liked the women, most of whom advocated "free love," and he liked the drugs—he started out on speed and then moved on to more dangerous drugs—that went along with the sex and the intellectual atmosphere that viewed music as the New Art.

In retrospect it seems odd that Jimmie didn't take Stevie into his home and introduce him to his friends in the music business, but their relationship had always been complicated, never more so than when the prodigal brother hit town determined to make his brother proud of him.

The differences between the brothers were highlighted when Stevie moved to Austin. Jimmie, who wore his hair slicked back into a 1950s-style pompadour, preferred cowboy hats and hard hats to hippie headbands and love beads. Although neither brother realized it at the time, Jimmie, with his intolerant attitude toward the hippies and his preference for blue-collar audiences, was becoming his father, and Stevie, with his inquiring mind and open heart, was becoming his mother.

In fact, those first few years in Austin brought about a reversal in the brothers' relationship. When Becky Crabtree told Stevie that her son Tyrone was Jimmie's son, Stevie let her live with him for a time, often baby-sitting Tyrone while she ran errands. If Jimmie didn't believe he was his son, Stevie certainly did, for he spoke lovingly of his "nephew" and spent time playing with him.

For most of his life, Stevie had heard bad things about Jimmie from his parents, about how he would never amount to anything and how Stevie, if he followed in his footsteps, would never amount to anything either. Stevie worshiped Jimmie, and it disturbed him greatly that people outside the family would bad-mouth him, which was essentially what Crabtree did by telling everyone that he was Tyrone's father. By acknowledging Tyrone as his nephew, Stevie stepped in and did the right thing as he saw it, thus mitigating criticism of his brother.

The other musicians in Austin greeted Stevie's arrival with great interest, for it conjured images of a wild-west shoot-out between the two brothers. That never happened because the brothers were not competitive in public, only in private. When Stevie played in Jimmie's band, each seemed careful not to outdo the other. It would have been difficult for them to compete on the same turf anyway, because their styles were so different.

Jimmie viewed music as a blank canvas, which he colored with carefully constructed rhythms and licks. He viewed the silence between those notes as a good thing. Stevie was just the opposite. He viewed music as an energy field that should completely cover the canvas. The more notes he hit in a given bar of music, the more fully he felt the energy field. Sometimes he grabbed hold of his music and rode it like a lightning bolt. Jimmie caressed his guitar. Stevie punched his guitar with both fists. Two brothers. Two styles. Two entirely different sounds.

During the early 1970s, neither brother had a consistent band. The players in Blackbird and Storm came and went. Both brothers lived day to day, hand to mouth, without much thought about what would happen tomorrow, much less next week or next month. There was no future, only the present.

After a brief time with Storm, Keith Ferguson joined Stevie in Blackbird, but that didn't last long because the band was already on its last legs. Stevie ended up joining a band named Krackerjack, a rock 'n' roll outfit that lived communally in a rambling two-story house on Sixteenth Street.

Most notable for its rhythm section, Uncle John Turner on drums and Tommy Shannon on guitar, both refugees from the Johnny Winter band, Krackerjack often seemed hell-bent on its own destruction. One of the band members came down with hepatitis. Soon after that Shannon and another band member were busted on drug charges. Stevie was fired from the band after he protested a suggestion that band members wear heavy theatrical makeup when they performed.

As crazy as the times were for Stevie, he found moments of ecstasy, such as the night he listened to Albert King perform in an Austin club. He heard that the Memphis guitar wizard was in town while he was performing somewhere else. After finishing his first set, he packed up his guitar and announced to his shocked audience that he was leaving to go listen to King. If they had any sense, he said, they would join him.

"By the time I got to Albert's gig, there were only about seventy-five people left in the place," he told *Guitar World*. "I ended up standing on a table right beside the stage, just staring at him throughout the whole set. Part way through the show he took his mic stand and walked over to where I was standing, planted it, and just stood there and sang and played to me the rest of the night. He didn't know me from Adam. I was just this skinny little kid, ninety-eight pounds soaking wet. I guess I must've yelled, 'Right!' or something. And when he finished playing he walked over to me, handed me his guitar and shook my hand. I was stunned."

Nights like that had a profound effect on Stevie. Faced by the realization that playing blues was what he really wanted to do—and frustrated because he understood that to be an effective bluesman, he would have to sing—he started drifting musically and emotionally. More ominously, he started shooting up with speed. His friends thought he was out of control and warned him about his drug use.

After playing with pickup bands for a while, he was asked to join his old friend Doyle Bramhall in a band named the Nightcrawlers. Bramhall didn't sing this time; he played drums. The singer was Marc Benno, who had made a name for himself as a songwriter for Leon Russell and the Dixie Flyers. He had recorded four albums for A&M Records and had hopes of recording a fifth. Actually, Stevie was not Benno's first choice as a guitarist. The Vaughan he really wanted was

Jimmie, but the older brother declined and suggested that he talk to Stevie, who didn't have any problem saying yes.

In April 1973, the Nightcrawlers flew to Los Angeles to record a new album for A&M. Stevie, then twenty-two, thought that he had made the big time. The record label put them all up in a good hotel and catered to their every whim. Unfortunately the recording session was a bust and A&M refused to release the album. Stevie returned to Austin, embarrassed and dejected. He had told everyone he was going to have a record. Now he would have to tell everyone the deal had fallen apart.

Without Benno, who had stayed in Los Angeles, the Nightcrawlers continued to perform in and around Austin. Once while visiting a friend in Corpus Christi, Stevie decided to get a tattoo. Instead of getting a tasteful (by music standards) design on his arm, he got the tattoo artist to do a giant eagle on his chest, with wings stretching from shoulder to shoulder. The process was so painful that his band mates had to hold him down, kicking and squirming the whole time, so that the tattoo artist could finish what he started. After that, Stevie lost all interest in getting additional tattoos.

Before the year was out, the Nightcrawlers attracted the attention of Bill Ham, the manager for the Texas rock group ZZ Top. He offered to set up a tour for the Nightcrawlers, with bookings that sent them as far east as Mississippi. The tour eventually ran into trouble, with the band frequently showing up for bookings that never existed or were canceled without notice. The "tour" ended in Jackson, Mississippi, with the band members broke and desperate for transportation back to Austin. When they returned, Ham was furious at them for breaking off the tour and he demanded that they reimburse him for the money he had spent.

That misadventure was the final straw for Stevie. Toward the end of 1974, he broke up the band and decided to give up music forever. He would get a day job and play music for himself. To hell with everyone else!

Stevie's self-imposed exile did not last long. In January 1974, he was asked to join a popular group called the Cobras. Since the band already had a lead guitarist named Denny Freeman, Stevie signed on as the second guitarist. He used his backseat position with the band to branch out in a new area—vocals. To everyone's surprise, he started singing, his scratchy voice tentative and coarse, but filled with what best could be called bemused passion. He tried to emulate the African American blues artists he admired, especially Bobby "Blue" Bland, who had one of the most distinctive voices around.

With the Cobras, Stevie recorded his first record, a single titled "Texas Clover/Other Days." The A-side, "Texas Clover" featured Freeman on guitar, while the flip side, "Other Days," featured Stevie. The record was a regional hit but attracted no attention from the major labels. During this time Stevie traded his 1963 Fender Stratocaster for a battered 1959 model with a rosewood fingerboard. It would remain his favorite guitar for the rest of his life.

In 1974 Kim Wilson was living in Minneapolis when a friend called him and suggested that he go to Austin to hear a blues band called Storm. The California native, who sang and played harmonica in a style perfected by Little Walter, had a band of his own, but it was going nowhere and he was eager to hook up with like-minded musicians who had his purist approach to the blues.

When Kim arrived in Austin, his friend introduced him to Stevie Vaughan and Doyle Bramhall, who agreed to take him to a black-owned rib joint named Alexander's, where Storm was booked for a Sunday matinee. When they arrived, Stevie asked if Kim could sit in with the band, but Jimmie said no. Not willing to take no for an answer, Stevie, Kim, and Doyle waited until the band took a break. Then, with the club owner's permission, they took the stage and played, driving the crowd "crazy," according to Kim's recollection in later years. Once Jimmie heard them, he joined them on stage, fascinated by Kim's wicked harmonica playing and his precise, under-played vocals. Jimmie almost didn't believe his own ears: Kim sang the way he played guitar.

Storm's singer, Lewis Cowdrey, was so angered by the impromptu performance that he quit the band that night, leaving Jimmie without a frontman. Kim stayed in town long enough to play harmonica on a recording session that never found a label and then returned to Minneapolis. Jimmie and Kim promised to stay in touch.

After Kim left town, Jimmie looked around for new band members, but everyone seemed to be taken. For about a month, he hung out at different clubs, looking for someone or something to spark his interest. He spent a lot of time at a club named Soap Creek, where Stevie was playing on a regular basis with the Cobras. He hadn't listened to Stevie in a long time and he was shocked at how good he had become. He was also shocked to see his kid brother step up to the microphone and sing an occasional song. Life would have been different for Jimmie, he knew, if only he had had the guts to sing.

Stevie seemed to be moving toward something good, but Jimmie felt his career had stalled. No one respected the blues, and that was all he wanted to play. The only blues bands that were making a living were playing more rock 'n' roll than blues—and they were playing it for college audiences that had never heard real blues.

At age twenty-three, Jimmie felt washed up and desperate. He picked up the telephone and called Kim, who invited him to Minneapolis to play guitar in his band. That lasted about three weeks. Homesick for Austin and his girlfriend, Connie, he returned home determined to make something out of his life, even if the first step meant getting married again (which he did).

There were plenty of rhythm-section possibilities in Austin—bass players and drummers were a dime a dozen and usually didn't particularly care what kind of music they played—but finding a singer who loved the blues as much as he did presented a formidable challenge to Jimmie. After a series of dead-end attempts to find a singer, Jimmie got on the telephone and begged Kim to come to Austin and put together a band with him. He promised him he would never be sorry.

That sounded good to Kim. Minneapolis was hardly the blues capital of the universe. Austin bore little resemblance to the Mississippi Delta, where the blues originated, but it did have a thriving nightclub scene that was more hip than most. Encouraged by Jimmie's vision for the future of the blues, Kim packed up everything he owned and headed south to Austin, where he moved into the house with Jimmie and his new wife Connie, who was reportedly not extremely happy about having a semipermanent house guest.

After going through a series of rhythm sections, Jimmie and Kim finally settled on Keith Ferguson on bass and Mike Buck on drums. They named the new band the Fabulous Thunderbirds and set out to ignite Austin audiences with their old-fashioned, some would say traditional, interpretations of the blues. Unfortunately, they quickly discovered that they could not readily locate an audience for their type of music.

In 1974 the situation in Austin was pretty much the same as it was elsewhere in the country. Black blues bands performed for black audiences and white rock bands performed for white audiences, even if they sometimes called their music the blues. The Fabulous Thunderbirds fit in neither category.

Jimmie and Kim were hanging out at a club one night, pondering their questionable future, when a dark-haired, long-legged young woman named Lou Ann Barton stepped up to the microphone and belted out a series of blues songs that left the two men practically quaking with excitement. She was obviously the solution to their problem. Nightclubs (black- or white-owned) that would not be caught dead with a white blues band would jump at the chance to have a white female blues singer. It was one of the musical quirks of the times: A good-looking white woman who could sing the blues was acceptable to everyone. It was that way all across the country.

That very night Jimmie and Kim asked Lou Ann Barton to join the band. True enough, bookings started rolling in, but the chemistry between Lou Ann and the other band members, especially Kim, who sometimes seemed threatened by her popularity, was too intense for that arrangement to last, so they fired her and went their separate ways despite the protestations of Ferguson, who was in love with her. Legend has it that Lou Ann's final day was so brutal that Kim could not sing for a week because his throat was raw from screaming at her.

For a time, the future looked bleak for the Fabulous Thunderbirds. It was difficult to get bookings and when they did, the crowds were usually small and unenthusiastic. With his thinning hair, round face, and restrained vocal style, Kim looked more like a crooning supermarket manager than a singing star. Jimmie looked like something out of a time machine, with his James Dean aura and his greased hair slicked back in a 1950s style.

The Fabulous Thunderbirds were a great band, but no one knew what to do with them. They probably would have faded into obscurity, a footnote in Austin music history, were it not for the efforts of a Lebanese grocery owner named Clifford Antone, who decided to open the city's first blues club. An aspiring bass player and admitted blues fan, he once cleaned out a backroom in his grocery and converted it into a place where he could play music with his friends. The Vaughan brothers, separately and sometimes together, often stopped by and jammed with Clifford all night and into the early hours of the morning.

In July 1975, Clifford's blues club—appropriately named Antone's—opened its doors, shocking local residents, many of whom considered the blues a dead art form played only by down-on-their-luck blacks in Mississippi and Memphis. Clifford's plan was to give local blues bands a performance venue and bring aging blues masters to the city so that people could see and hear the real thing.

The Fabulous Thunderbirds were asked to be one of two unofficial house bands at the club, a stroke of good fortune that prevented the breakup of the group. Even better than having a regular gig was the opportunity it offered them to back up some of the blues legends that performed in the club.

One of their most memorable encounters was with Muddy Waters. As the opening act, the Fabulous Thunderbirds were expected to warm up the crowd for the grand master. "We wanted to play good stuff, but we didn't want to play *his* stuff—not in front of him," Jimmie told Margaret Moser in an interview for the *Austin Chronicle*. "We got to one song. I forget which it was, but I did the Earl Hooker slide thing. I saw the dressing room curtain upstairs pull back and it was like, 'Gulp!' The next night Muddy came down and walked behind the stage and grabbed me around the neck. He liked it! Later that night he told me, 'When I'm not here, I want you to do that. Show people how I did that.'" Muddy Waters was so taken by Kim's harmonica playing that he told him he could have a job with his band anytime he wanted one.

When Muddy Waters left to tour through the Northeast, he told everyone about the Fabulous Thunderbirds. He liked the fact that they were a white band that played the blues as it was originally envisioned. They didn't wear hippie headbands or try to jazz the music up with rock licks. They just played it from the heart, pure and simple.

With Muddy Waters spreading the word, it wasn't long before booking agents in the East started calling the Fabulous Thunderbirds with offers for work. Their first tour took them to New York and then on to Canada. Jimmie and Kim were ecstatic to be on the road, but drummer Mike Buck and bass player Keith Ferguson were not so happy about the tour. It was Mike's first time out on the road and he didn't particularly care for it, and Keith missed his girlfriend Lou Ann Barton, who used his absence as an excuse to move in with another musician (Keith and Lou Ann later got married).

The band successfully completed the New York part of the tour, but before they headed up to Canada, Mike told them he had had enough. He quit the band and went back to Austin, leaving them without a drummer for the remaining bookings.

Fran Christina was training a horse at his isolated Nova Scotia farm when a couple of Canadian Mounties rode onto his property. "You Fran Christina?" asked one of the Mounties.

"Yeah, who's asking?"

"The Fabulous Thunderbirds want you to meet them in London, Ontario."

With that, the stoic Mounties said "Good day" and rode off into the midmorning sun. Fran was stunned by the encounter. He had no idea that Mounties delivered messages, especially to blues drummers. He was speechless. Besides, while he had heard of the Fabulous Thunderbirds, he had never met them or heard them perform.

At that time (1975), Fran was better known than any of the Fabulous Thunderbirds. After teaching himself to play drums when he was twelve, he and a few high-school friends, including Duke Robillard and Al Copely, formed a band when they were only sixteen. Roomful of Blues went on to become one of the premier blues bands on the East Coast.

From Roomful of Blues, Fran branched out in the late 1960s and early 1970s to play with blues legends such as Mighty Joe Young, Johnny Shines, and Big Walter Horton, and with popular bands such as the Vipers and the Rhythm Rockers. In 1975, when the Mounties showed up, he was enjoying a much-needed break.

When Fran and his wife got married in 1971, they went to Nova Scotia, fell in love with the place, and bought a farm. The culture was not too different from what he was used to growing up in Rhode

Island—the East Coast is still the East Coast, whether you live in the United States or Canada—but there was more space in Nova Scotia, more room to live in relative isolation from the noise and pressures of the city.

Fran's farm was so isolated that he did not even have a telephone, which was why the Mounties delivered the message to him. "I was living in the woods," recalls Fran. "No electricity, no running water—there was nothing there to do with the outside world."

Not one to turn down a plea for help from fellow musicians, Fran hitchhiked from Nova Scotia to London, Ontario, a distance of about 1,800 miles. When he arrived at the club where the Fabulous Thunderbirds were supposed to play, there was no one there, so he sat down on the steps and waited. He had been there all day when the T-Birds drove up in their road-scarred van.

"The door throws open and Keith Ferguson, who had on boa constrictor boots up to his knees and hair down his back and smelling like a bottle of Jade East, steps out," says Fran. "Then Jimmie and Kim get out of the van and I look at them and they look at me and I looked like a lumberjack. I had a beard and long hair, and I had on a Pendleton woolen shirt, and they said, 'Are you the drummer?' And I said, 'Yeah, you the band?'"

After exchanging pleasantries, they unloaded the gear and set up inside the club. Fran wanted to know why they contacted him. They explained that when their drummer cut out and returned to Austin before the tour ended, they contacted other bands they knew and asked for suggestions for a replacement. A member of the Texas swing band Asleep at the Wheel recommended that they track down Fran Christina in Nova Scotia.

"I had heard about them, but I had never heard them," says Fran. "But after we started playing, it was like we had played together for a hundred years. It was magic. It all clicked."

Asked about his first impression of Jimmie nearly thirty years later, Fran laughed and said that the guitarist smelled like a hooker. "You've got to realize that I just came out of the woods and I had nothing to do with cologne or aftershave," he explained. "When you live back in the woods and you don't have a lot of contact with other people, manmade smells are the first thing that your senses grab onto. That was the most rudimentary thing that struck me, but when Jimmie started playing was something else. I was like, 'This is it! The guy's rockin'! The band's rockin'!' He knew exactly where he was coming from. I just loved him."

After performing that night, the T-Birds returned to Austin and Fran hitchhiked back to his farm in Nova Scotia.

The T-Bird's tour impressed Stevie mightily. Each step that Jimmie took in the direction of the Big Time bolstered Stevie's confidence that he could follow. He was competitive with his older brother, but it was not a nihilistic competition. He wanted his brother to succeed because that meant that he too could succeed.

Meanwhile, he soaked up every musical influence he thought might be of use. One of his heroes at that point was Stax recording artist Albert King, probably best known for songs such as "Crosscut Saw," "Born under a Bad Sign," and "As Years Go Passing By."

When Stevie learned that King was booked at Antone's, he pestered Clifford on a daily basis to give him information about his hero's arrival. As a result, when King's bus pulled up outside the club, Stevie was waiting there for him. Before King took the stage, Clifford asked the guitarist if he would mind if Steve sat in with him for a song or two.

That wasn't the sort of thing that most club owners would have the nerve to ask an artist of King's caliber, but Clifford was new to the business and King seemed to take that into account. Fine, he said—let's see what the boy can do. Embarrassed by the attention, Stevie took the stage and never looked up from his shoes as he gave it his best shot. King was so impressed with Stevie's playing that he allowed him to stay on the stage with him for the remainder of the night. No matter what string of notes King played on his Flying V guitar, Stevie had an answer for it.

The two men parted company that night, with King convinced that he had shared the stage with one of the most talented white blues musicians he had ever encountered, and Stevie convinced that he had walked among the gods.

When Jimmie and the T-Birds returned to Austin, Stevie began to get restless with the progress—or lack of it—he was making in the

Cobras. It really wasn't a tight family. The other members didn't seem very ambitious to him and they thought that he was too spastic and too young to appreciate what they wanted to do with their music. Stevie was always reaching, always playing all over the place, and they had a sense of order that he sometimes stumbled into like a bull in a china closet.

Impressed by Jimmie's progress, Stevie left the Cobras in 1976 to form a band of his own. He wanted to sing and he wanted to take chances with his music. He wanted to show Jimmie that he wasn't simply spinning his wheels. On drums, he went with Fredde Pharoah, a veteran who had played with the Storm. Mike Kindred, a former member of Krackerjack, was asked to play keyboards, and W. C. Clark, a black soul singer, was recruited to play bass and do some vocals.

Although it was his intention to sing more songs himself, Stevie knew he couldn't front the band as a singer. For that job he appealed to Lou Ann Barton. They named the five-member band the Triple Threat Revue, a name that confused people who wondered exactly who the three threats were supposed to be.

The band was well received in Austin and soon landed bookings in other Texas cities, providing them with a busy schedule; but music is never enough to hold a group together and it soon became evident that Triple Threat's greatest weakness were the personalities of the individual band members.

Barton hated it when Stevie stole her thunder with blistering guitar solos. Stevie, who was reportedly sleeping with her at the time, felt the same way about her vamping it up over his playing and he often became angry when she flirted with the audience. Stevie and Barton argued constantly, often in the presence of the audience. Playing bass was Clark's least favorite thing to do—he wanted to sing more—so conflicts arose over the vocal balances. And so it went.

After less than a year, the band bailed on Stevie and Barton. In the spring of 1978, Stevie and Barton formed a new band they named Double Trouble (after Stevie's favorite Otis Rush song). It featured Jackie Newhouse on bass, Johnny Reno on saxophone, and newcomer Chris Layton on drums.

Following in Jimmie's footsteps, Stevie insisted that the band do as many gigs on the road as possible. Sidemen didn't like that because it meant less money for them to divide up among themselves, but for musicians with ambitions of stardom (Stevie and Barton), less money was viewed as a necessary sacrifice to build up an audience.

Living expenses were not a huge problem for Stevie because he got in the habit, early in his career, of living with women who had day jobs. Whenever he argued with a girlfriend, which tended to be often, he would take his sleeping bag and portable record player and crash at a friend's house. He lived like a gypsy whose eyes were always in the clouds searching for the Big Score.

It was around this time that Stevie met a dark-eyed, olive-skinned beauty named Lenora Bailey. Lenny—she preferred that people call her by her nickname—was involved with someone else at the time, but Stevie fell for her in a big way and started seeing her on the side. She was like Stevie in a lot of ways—wild and unpredictable and hungry for something in life that she couldn't quite put her finger on. But she was better educated (she could speak fluent German) and she could fit in with the straight world that always seemed so alien to Stevie. On top of all that, she was a real beauty: She was once selected Miss Copperas Cove (the name of a small town near Fort Hood).

One day, after Lenny had a fight with her boyfriend, she ran into Stevie in a restaurant and boldly asked him to move in with her. He went home with her that night and wrote a song titled "Love Struck"—and later told the guys in his band that he was seriously in love. They took that information with a grain of salt because Stevie was always seriously in love; defying all the odds, it turned out to be true this time.

In late December 1979, before performing at a nightclub named the Rome Inn, Stevie proposed marriage to Lenny. She said yes, surprising everyone, including herself. Between sets that evening, a preacher who was hastily summoned from the Yellow Pages of the local telephone book married them. They cemented their proclamations of undying love with rings fashioned from pieces of metal found on the floor of the nightclub.

"The wedding was pretty spontaneous," Chris Layton later recalled to VH1. "It wasn't like it had been planned for weeks in advance. It was like, 'Hey, let's get married. Here, I got this wire, we'll, I'll make some rings, and, uh, let's do it.'"

There was something equally spontaneous about the band. Nothing ever seemed contrived. The music flowed from the bandstand as if tapped from some hidden, subterranean spring of blues power. The only negative energy came from the fiery interplay between Stevie and Barton. There are few bands that can maintain more than one "star" at a time—the Beatles being perhaps the most successful at that—and it was just a matter of time before the Stevie–Barton tension tore the band apart.

Their final performance occurred in 1980 at the Lone Star in New York City. "We booked them for one hundred dollars," Cleve Hattersley told *Guitar World*. "They drove all the way up from Austin and crashed on friends' couches. The gig went all right, but afterward, Lou Ann kind of got out of hand. She was real drunk, and threw beer glasses and screamed at the waitresses. And Stevie, of course, was upset."

The next day, Barton announced that she was leaving Double Trouble to sing with Roomful of Blues. Stevie returned to Austin, not certain what to do about replacing Barton. He either had to find a new singer or start fronting the band himself. He wasn't sure he could pull it off—and neither was anyone else.

For the first time since childhood Stevie felt musically adrift. On the first night that he fronted for his new band, he and Lenny were arrested for cocaine possession in Houston by an off-duty policeman who witnessed the couple having too much fun backstage with a white powder.

When they went to court, both pleaded guilty to cocaine possession. Lenny got five years' probation and Stevie got two years' probation, with the added requirement that he undergo drug treatment and avoid "disreputable" characters. He underwent the treatment, with no positive results—and the part about avoiding disreputable characters was a joke because *all* of his musician friends fell in that category.

The cocaine bust was a wake-up call that Stevie slept straight through.

In April 1980, Stevie and Double Trouble performed at an Austin nightclub named Steamboat 1874. What made the performance different, besides the fact that Stevie did all the vocals, was the fact that radio station KGSR-FM was there to broadcast the hour-long performance live. If that bothered Stevie, he never let on that it did. He and the other band members figured that it could be the big break that they needed.

Wearing a sleeveless T-shirt and a tan cap—and avoiding any initial chat with the audience—Stevie launched into Freddie King's "In the Open," a hot-shuffle instrumental with a frenetic guitar solo. Without a word between songs, the band then went to one of Stevie's compositions, "Slide Thing," an instrumental with more traditional blues phrasing, though Stevie did make his strings scream from time to time.

Not until the third song, "They Call Me Guitar Hurricane," did Stevie step up to the microphone and introduce himself and the other band members. Then he delivered his first vocal. His voice was energetic, without pretense, and slipped nicely into the groove of what was essentially an old-fashioned rock 'n' roll stomper.

Without waiting for applause, he began Otis Rush's "All Your Love," singing with surprising confidence, as if he had been doing it for years. Next came "Tin Pan Alley," a slow blues number for which he blended a growling vocal punctuated with deliberately wicked guitar licks. It was clear that he was experimenting with his voice, trying at times to sound black and at other times to just be himself.

Not until after "Shake for Me," did Stevie attempt to talk to the audience. "Hope you're enjoying yourself tonight," he said. Then, feeling like he perhaps had said too much, he started into another one of his compositions, "Live Another Day."

Most of the performance was recorded on multitrack and two-track recorders. The entire show was not recorded because the tape ran out before Stevie finished playing. After the show, KGSR-FM program director Wayne Bell, who hosted the show, asked the band if they wanted the tapes, but no one showed any interest.

The radio station kept the multitrack master tape for a few weeks, in case Stevie claimed it, but when no one stepped forward, the tape was destroyed. Bell kept the two-track tape in his personal library and it was not heard again until 1992, when it was titled *In the Beginning* and released by Epic Records on CD. Although it took a song or two for the sound engineer to find a proper level for Jackie Newhouse's bass parts, it is an amazingly solid recording, showing Stevie at his early best.

Not long after that, Stevie was performing in Houston when an old acquaintance, Tommy Shannon, stopped by to visit after reading about the performance in the newspaper. Down on his luck, Shannon had done some jail time and was working as a bricklayer in Houston. One thing led to another, and Shannon sat in with Double Trouble, rekindling the old fire he had experienced with Stevie in Krackerjack.

"I remember I walked in and it was like a revelation," Shannon told Art Tipaldi of the *Dallas Observer*. "Something just hit me right between the eyes, and I knew that's where I belonged. I said, 'That's where I belong.' And I told Stevie that. I had never done anything like that in my life. I'm not ashamed of it. I said, 'Stevie, I belong in this band with you.' And I didn't care who was listening. I had to say it."

Two weeks later, Stevie fired Newhouse and replaced him on bass with Shannon, thus creating the rhythm section of Double Trouble that would see him all the way through to the apocalypse.

When the Fabulous Thunderbirds returned to Austin from Canada, minus Fran Christina, who went back to Nova Scotia, they hooked back up with drummer Mike Buck and got serious about their future as a band. Energized by their East Coast tour, they realized that they had a future as a road band—and hopefully as recording artists.

They still played in Austin, but they increasingly looked beyond the city to find new audiences. "For a long time, we doubled up in rooms and traveled in a van," says Kim Wilson. "When you put 100,000 miles on a van in six months, the warranty runs out. But it was a lot of fun. We had great times and gained a lot of experience, things you don't learn in school." He paused, grinning broadly. "I would say, stay in school," he laughed. "I can look back on so many different moments, so many people we worked with—Muddy Waters, Jimmy Reed—it was fantastic. If you can have that and what your mother could call success, that's great."

After nearly four years of one-nighters from one side of the country to the other, they finally landed a record deal with Maryland-based Takoma Records. In May 1979, when the Village People were topping the charts with "In the Navy" and the Sex Pistols with "Silly Thing," the T-Birds went into a studio to record an album of blues songs.

Produced by Denny Bruce, the self-titled album, which was sub-titled *Girls Go Wild,* contained several songs penned by Kim Wilson and several traditional blues songs, such as Slim Harpo's "Scratch My Back" and Jerry McCain's "She's Tuff." In 1979 McCain was about as obscure as a blues artist could be and still make a living. Born in Alabama, he seldom ventured further away from home than Jackson, Mississippi, where he made his recording debut in 1952 on the Trumpet label. The T-Birds was the most famous unknown band at that point in his career to ever record his music.

"Scratch My Back" was one of the more interesting songs on the album. Mostly an instrumental (Kim spoke a few lyrics every verse or so), it featured Kim on blues harp and Jimmie playing his guitar so that it would sound like a chicken.

The most soulful song on the album was "Full-Time Lover," a blues ballad with an old-time feel of the type made famous by Bobby "Blue" Bland and others. Kim seemed to intone the song's lyrics with the same intensity Bland used in "Stormy Monday Blues."

The album was built entirely around Kim's harp playing and Jimmie's determined guitar rhythms and crystal-clear phrasing whenever he played lead. That type of music was so far out of the mainstream that it is amazing that they were able to find a record label willing to release it.

Unfortunately, finding a label that is both willing to record your album and able to promote and distribute it is doubly challenging. The album never sold because Takoma had no way of effectively locating a market for it. Record stores purchased records that were being played on the radio. At that time, black radio stations were not enthusiastic about playing records recorded by white bands and white stations were not interested in the blues. That left albums such as *Girls Go Wild* with no place to go.

Nonetheless, the Fabulous Thunderbirds now had a record that they could talk about on the bandstand, a distinction that gave the band added credibility with nightclub audiences, which were growing larger with each passing year. At that time, there seemed to be a parallel universe when it came to music. There was radio music, morning-drive elixir dominated by the pop stylists who drove record and concert sales—and there was club music, the darker, heart-to-soul concoction that people wanted to listen to on their evenings off and wash down with a couple of cold beers.

The Fabulous Thunderbirds were the master of their domain when it came to club music—few bands could touch them in the late 1970s—but the band was barely making expenses and the members had bills to pay.

Most of the time, Jimmie, Kim, Keith, and Mike loved each other, walking in lockstep to do battle with the universe; but there were times when they were at each other's throats. Fistfights before and after gigs between Jimmie and Kim, and Kim and Keith were commonplace, creating an atmosphere of imminent self-destruction. There was always another shoe to drop—and working together was sometimes like living with a schizophrenic who may or may not throw a plate of food during any given meal on any given day. Anything could happen.

Not long after their debut album was released, the band could see that it would not be a success. Fortunately for the T-Birds, Chrysalis Records bought out Takoma Records and took an immediate interest in the band. In 1980 the record label asked Denny Bruce to produce another album.

Bruce called Kim and asked if they had any new songs, and Kim assured him that they did and that they were eager to go into the studio again. "Wait 'till you get here," Kim told him, as reported in the liner notes, "We got some wild shit you're gonna dig."

For the album, which they titled *What's the Word?*, they gathered five songs written by Kim, two written by Kim and Jimmie, and one song written by Jimmie and Keith Ferguson. The remaining four songs were covers of traditional, 1950s blues and blues-rock songs.

"Running Shoes," the first cut on the album, was a remake of a tune written and recorded by Weldon "Juke Boy" Bonner, a Jimmy Reed imitator who died two years before the T-Birds recorded his song. Kim did some good harmonica work on it, but Jimmie allowed his guitar to fade into the background as he did on "Low-Down Woman," one of Kim's compositions.

"You Ain't Nothing but Fine," written by Rockin' Sydney Simien, has an early rock 'n' roll feel to it, but Kim plays the solo instead of Jimmie in keeping with Simien's zydeco approach to the song. Jimmie's guitar work was almost invisible.

They included three instrumentals on the album—"Extra Jimmies," "Last Call for Alcohol," and "Jumpin' Bad"—all written by Jimmie with either Keith or Kim, but overall Jimmie had few guitar solos. Jimmie's best guitar work was on "Last Call for Alcohol," which had him bouncing from rhythm to bursts of delicate solo notes.

Jimmie was able to rock back and forth between rhythm and solos because he used a capo, a clamp that fits over the neck and constricts the strings in such a manner that a guitar player can always play in the key of E. "For blues, it helps me with pull-offs and my saxophone-style phrasing," he once explained to *Guitar One*. "For soloing, it helps me to stop and 'get in the moment.'"

The only song on the album that approached a ballad tempo was Kim's composition, "Dirty Work." He had a real knack for writing material that imitated the phrasing and sentiments of traditional blues songs. Some musicians couldn't tell his songs from the ones written by the blues masters, a fact that always amused him. In previous bands, he would sing one of his compositions; when asked who wrote it, he would sometimes attribute it to Muddy Waters or Jimmy Reed, a ruse that seemed to make his songs more appreciated by his bandmates.

What's the Word? was recorded at Sumet Burnet Studios in Dallas, one of the best equipped in Texas. It had an expansive, forty-foot ceiling that measured sixty-five by fifty feet, large enough to accommodate an entire orchestra. During that time, three additional songs were recorded live at an Austin bar named The Bottom Line, with the view of including them on the album. Although the live material failed to make the cut, it was included by Benchmark Records when it rereleased the album in 2000.

In some ways, the album was one of the most contentious ever recorded by the T-Birds. Midway through the sessions, the band decided to replace Mike Buck on drums. They got in touch with Fran Christina, who had moved to Texas from Nova Scotia in 1978 to play with Asleep at the Wheel.

Fran was delighted to rejoin the T-Birds. The inspired gig he had played with them in London, Ontario, had provided the impetus to move to Texas. He slipped onto Mike's drum stool before it even had time to cool.

"Musically, it was just completely comfortable for me because it was the music that I loved, the music that I grew up with," Fran explained. "It was alive. It wasn't being treated like something in a museum. If we didn't have it in three takes, then we got rid of it and went on to something else. It was easy and comfortable and there were fireworks. Things were happening. You would think you were hearing something that had been played before, then Jimmie would throw in one of his wild hairs and it was something new. Keith played like his bass was another percussion instrument. Everything fit like a glove."

When *What's the Word?* was released, it contained six songs with Mike Buck on drums and six songs with Fran Christina on drums. Even a novice musician could hear the difference in the two styles. Mike was more of a slap drummer, evoking the steady, flat sounds of the early blues players, while Fran had a more innovative rock 'n' roll style that utilized dramatic rolls and change-of-pace rhythms.

When the album was released in 1980, it bumped heads with a pop market that included artists such as Genesis, Judas Priest, and Blondie (another Chrysalis recording artist). Blues fans appreciated the album, but mainstream America simply wasn't interested in a roots sound at that time. The album boosted the T-Birds' ego and exalted their status as a bar band, but it did little to fill their wallets.

CHAPTER 3

Butt Rockin' into
a Texas Flood

A S THE 1980s began, Stevie Ray Vaughan and Double Trouble alternated with the Fabulous Thunderbirds in the minds of Texas music lovers as the best bar bands in the state. Of course, neither band was making much money. Each time either band set up in a barroom for another night of music, it was about bragging rights as much as anything—and making enough money to exist another twenty-four hours.

Actually, with two albums to promote, the Fabulous Thunderbirds received more recognition than Stevie's band and landed more offers to tour out of the state. In 1980 and 1981, Stevie Ray Vaughan and Double Trouble ventured to the West Coast once and the East Coast twice. Mostly they traveled back and forth between barroom gigs in Austin, Houston, Lubbock, and Dallas, playing venues in which Stevie could be comfortable learning to front the band as its vocalist.

"We were like a family," Tommy Shannon told the *Dallas Observer*. "Stevie was not the kind of person who liked to be on his own. We'd do anything for each other. Most important, we all had a common goal and drive. Chris's and my role was to play the best we could for Stevie. Stevie never played anything the same way twice, unless it was the main riff of the song or something. But he would just all of a sudden go to a change knowing we'd be right there. He wouldn't turn around and tell anybody. Sometimes I'd do a bass line running down, walk down and get it to go right down with him. So it was like this intuitive thing we were doing."

Stevie moved easily into the role of the band's frontman, stretching his voice in directions he never knew it could go. He had a good bluesman's voice and he stuck to the material he knew he could handle, and in time his voice became as distinctive as his guitar riffs. His biggest problem during this period was deciding whether he wanted to play blues or Jimi Hendrix–style rock 'n' roll.

Often he mixed the two styles (usually to the displeasure of his audience). When he was in his Hendrix mode, he turned up his amps as high as they would go and experimented with distortion and mind-twisting riffs that had a frantic energy to them. The only problem with mixing blues and high-octane rock was that they appealed to two different audiences.

In June 1982, Stevie and the band were booked at the City Coliseum in Austin as an opening act for the British punk band, Clash. They had scored several Top 20 hits in England in the early 1980s, including "Bank Robber" and "London Calling," but the band's record label, CBS Records, had been hesitant to release their records in the United States, despite the fact that the band's records were import best-sellers.

The Clash 1982 American tour was organized in support of a single, "Rock the Casbah," which went on to become a Top 20 hit on American charts. When the opportunity came to book Stevie's band as the opening act, his management jumped at the opportunity. There was no money in the blues, but there was plenty of money in the type of music that Clash was cashing in on.

Stevie and the band members were reluctant to accept the booking because, blues–rock purists that they were, they didn't want to be associated with a British punk band. Management pointed out that it was a sold-out show and would be great publicity for them. Reluctantly they agreed to perform two nights as the opening act.

The first night turned out to be a nightmare. As soon as they walked out on the stage, they were booed. They figured it would get better once the music started, but it didn't. No only did the irate audience boo them, individual members threw things at them and shouted at them to go home. Shaken by the hostility, Stevie and the band completed the set but refused to perform on the second night.

The following month, still bruised over the Clash fiasco, they left the country for the first time to perform at the Montreux Jazz Festival in Switzerland. It was a rarity for an unknown, unsigned band to perform at the festival, but a well-known American rhythm and blues record producer named Jerry Wexler had recommended the band to promoters after hearing them in Texas.

Convinced that the festival would help them get a record deal, they jumped at the chance to go, even though they had to borrow $15,000 from their management company to pay their travel expenses. Shannon had played the festival in 1969, when he went as a member of the Johnny Winters band, and he had nothing but good things to say about it. Even though neither Stevie nor Layton had ever been out of the country, they were excited about the prospect of performing in Europe, for it meant that finally they were headed for the big time.

By the time they arrived in Geneva, Switzerland, they were pumped with emotion, convinced they were destined to be heralded as conquering heroes. Backstage, before going on, they ran into Larry Graham, the Texas-born bass player for Sly and the Family Stone. To Shannon's delight, Graham asked if he could jam with them when they played their encore.

By that time, Layton was beginning to have some misgivings, despite all the excitement. "I noticed that there hadn't been any other electric bands up until we went on," he told *Guitar Player*. "It occurred to me that we were going to be quite a contrast—Stevie had a couple of amps up there, and we always played loud—but it never entered our minds that we might not go over."

Blues bands had played the festival before, but they had all been low-key bands that used minimum amplification, so as not to contrast too vividly with the acoustic jazz groups that set the tone and pace at the festival.

When Stevie and Double Trouble performed that day, they played at full volume, sending a wall of sound out into the audience that was turned back on them in the form of loud boos and hisses. It was a rematch of what had happened in Austin with Clash. Stevie was stunned, for that was the last thing he had expected, but he played the full set.

When Stevie walked off stage, he was in tears. He retreated to a dark corner, where he slumped over a roadcase, his dreams of stardom shattered. Blues legend John Hammond Jr., who was there to perform, sought Stevie out and apologized to him for the way the crowd reacted. He told him that it was just one of those things, that everyone knew how good he and his band were.

Of course, the band was not called back for an encore, which meant that Shannon never got to perform with Graham, an embarrassment that haunted him for years. "The first thing I heard Stevie say was 'I didn't think we were that bad,'" Shannon told *USA Today*. "He was very hurt, as we all were. If you listen to his playing that night [a reference to the CD that was subsequently released] you can feel the pain in it. Whatever he was feeling and thinking came through in his music."

Being booed as an opening act for Clash was one thing, but what happened to Stevie that day in Geneva was something else. He had felt knife-twisting pain before, especially growing up in Dallas, but never had he encountered the level of pain he felt on the stage that day. Music was what protected him from the pain of life; for that protection to fail him in such a public way was devastating.

Ironically, from that train wreck of a performance two events emerged that would change his life. In the audience that day were David Bowie and Jackson Browne. Bowie had gone to the performance specifically to hear Stevie and his band. Unlike the crowd, he was blown away by what he heard. After the show, Bowie sought out Stevie and they talked about a new project that Bowie had planned. Bowie told him that he would love for him to make a cameo on his next video.

Browne also talked to Stevie after the show. He was so impressed by the band that he told Stevie that they could use his Los Angeles studio free of charge anytime they wanted to make a record. It was a generous offer that Stevie interpreted as validation of his potential as a recording artist.

When Stevie and the band returned to Austin, they were hailed as conquering heroes. No one seemed concerned that they had been booed off the stage. They had played at the festival, and that was enough. For the next few weeks after their return to Texas, they enjoyed one sold-out performance after another.

Encouraged, Stevie called Jackson Browne and accepted his offer of studio time. Brown told him that he could have three days of recording time during the slow days around Thanksgiving. Working day and night, with Texan Richard Mullen as the engineer, they recorded ten songs—six originals and four covers. The last song they recorded was "Texas Flood," a hypnotic blues ballad written by Oklahoma bluesman Larry Davis. The album was pretty much recorded live because there was time for only two overdubs, both done because Stevie broke a guitar string.

While they were in the studio, Stevie received a telephone call from David Bowie, who wanted to know if Stevie would come to New York to play on his new album. Stevie was ecstatic. The two men were into two radically different types of music, but each knew that he had something the other needed. Bowie needed fire and passion on his album, and Stevie needed name recognition. No question: It was a done deal.

Bowie had told his producer, Nile Rodgers, that he wanted Stevie to play on his next album, *Let's Dance,* immediately after the Montreux Jazz Festival, but it took a while to set the wheels in motion.

When they started working together at the Power Station in New York, Rodgers couldn't understand why Bowie was so excited about Stevie. If Bowie wanted a blues guitarist on his album, he wondered, why didn't he just get someone like Albert King? As the session progressed, Rodgers changed his mind and became a true fan.

Stevie was never certain exactly what Bowie had in mind. He just played when and where asked by Rodgers. "What I did was go in there and get the best tone I could out of the amp without blowing it up, which I did do to the first one—I killed it," Stevie told the *Dallas Times-Herald.* "But I finally realized just to go in there and play like I play and it would fit. I'd never played on anything like that before, but I just played like I play and it worked."

Bowie, who produced the album with Rodgers, was impressed. "Stevie strolled into the [studio] and proceeded to rip up everything one thought about dance records," Bowie told *Guitar Player.* "He knocked down solo upon solo, and pulled notes out of the air that no one could have dreamed would work with my songs. In a ridiculously short time, he had become midwife to the sound that had been ringing in my ears all year."

When *Let's Dance* was released, it proved to be Bowie's bestselling album ever, out doing his previous bestseller, *Ziggy Stardust* by more than 3 million copies. Many people, Bowie included, attributed the success of the album, in part, to Stevie's raw-edged guitar style. Not surprisingly, Bowie asked Stevie to tour with him the following year. Stevie agonized over accepting the offer, fearing that it would signal a sellout of his blues roots, but he ended up saying yes, optimistic that it would help launch his own career.

When Stevie showed up for rehearsals, it was obvious that his involvement in the tour was going to be troublesome to everyone, himself included. He didn't get along well with the band director because he couldn't read music. That situation was aggravated by Stevie's wife, Lenny, who made a nuisance of herself and further annoyed the band director, who thought that she was a bad influence. As a result, Lenny was banned from the rehearsals.

Bowie tried to make up for that by asking Double Trouble to be the opening act for the tour. That made everyone happy (except perhaps Lenny), but the further they got into the details, the worse it looked. Bowie's management made it clear that Double Trouble would not be able to promote itself outside the tour for the duration.

One thing led to another and Stevie ended up walking away from the tour.

Everyone thought that he was crazy, himself included, but he was emboldened by the tracks that he and the band had recorded at Browne's studio. They sent them to John Hammond, who promised to try to get them a record deal. Those tracks were Stevie's secret weapon. He figured it was just a matter of time before he had a recording contract—and a big league tour—of his own. David Bowie could just kiss his Texas butt.

With two albums under their belt, the Fabulous Thunderbirds worked the road for all it was worth. Before finishing *What's the Word?*, they went to England to tour with Rockpile, a British group led by Dave Edmunds, an ardent T-Birds fan. When they returned to the States, it was with a new sense of importance for their music. The problem with playing night after night in Austin bars was that it tended to dull their appreciation of their music's worldwide appeal. Their trip to England, where the blues is revered as an art form, recharged their dreams.

With Fran Christina on drums, they were again a family: All for one and one for all. Unfortunately that sense of family did not extend to Jimmie and Stevie, who were somewhat estranged. Stevie was jealous of Jimmie's two albums, and Jimmie was uncomfortable with the attention that his baby brother was getting without any albums to his credit. Besides that, Jimmie was not happy with the direction Stevie was taking with his playing. He hated it when Stevie thought he was Jimi Hendrix and emulated his psychedelic guitar riffs.

"I think at that time they had not spoken in two years," recalled Fran, who got to know Stevie when he first moved to Texas. "You know, they were typical brothers—they loved each other, no doubt about it, but they also got into their spats and sometimes wouldn't see each other for six months or a year."

In 1981, when Chrysalis Records gave them approval to do another album, they decided to leave Texas and record at Crystal Studios in Hollywood, California. They wanted a slicker, fuller sound, something that would be more attractive to radio. Because they also wanted to add more punch, they invited members of Fran's old band, Roomful of Blues: Al Copley on piano, Greg Piccolo on tenor sax, Doug James on baritone sax.

Kim contributed six of the eleven songs on *Butt Rockin'*. One of his songs, "I Believe I'm in Love," was the first cut on the album and featured Kim on his harmonica, with a pounding piano rhythm in the background.

Another one of Kim's compositions, "Give Me All Your Lovin'," had a 1950s feel to it and made good use of the Roomful of Blues horn section. Jimmie played a solo on this song, a rarity since Kim often wrote his songs with a harmonica solo in mind.

The best mix of horns, piano, vocals, and guitar solos on the album occurred on "Roll, Roll, Roll," an up-tempo number on which Jimmie delivered his best recorded solo to date, an uncluttered riff that tore right through the rhythm of the song.

This album also included one of the most unusual songs the T-Birds ever recorded, "Cherry Pink and Apple Blossom White." Jimmie had listened to Perez Prado's version of the song at his parents' home in the mid-1950s when it was the number 1 record in America for two straight months. It was knocked to number 2 by Bill Haley and the Comets' "Rock around the Clock," thus signaling the dawn of a new era.

"It's a song everybody knows," Jimmie explained in the liner notes. "A couple of years back, we were playing in front of a small crowd, and there were three of four older people there who requested it. We did it, and we have kept doing it since then."

Kim liked the song, which they played as an instrumental because it allowed him to show his stuff on harmonica. The T-Bird version, which had a distinctly Tex-Mex flavor, had Kim blowing lots of sustained notes and Jimmie playing a guitar part that he apparently lifted right from a 1958 record titled "Tequila," the first rock 'n' roll instrumental ever to go to number 1 on the charts.

In 2000 Benchmark Records rereleased *Butt Rockin'* with several bonus tracks (songs that were recorded at the session but not put on the original album). That's a shame, because one of the bonus tracks, "Found a New Love," which Kim wrote, is one of the best songs on the album. A ballad, it is the only track on which horns and piano were put to maximum use.

Kim Wilson is an extraordinary songwriter who has never received the recognition he deserves for his writing skills. He has a knack for tuning into 1950s music, both lyrically and instrumentally, to the point where his material is often better than the material he emulates.

The Fabulous Thunderbirds had high hopes for *Butt Rockin'*. They held the release party at downtown Austin's Paramount Theater. Jimmie invited Stevie to open the show, but he declined by explaining that he now played for a rock 'n' roll crowd and he didn't think their blues audience would appreciate his music.

Two years earlier, it would have been unthinkable for one Vaughan brother to decline opening for the other, but pressures of success and different directions in music had driven a wedge between the brothers. There was always an element of sibling rivalry, but it was cloaked in Stevie's adulation of his brother and it was always expressed verbally with good-natured sparring.

Now that they each had attracted national attention, it was every man for himself.

The following year, Chrysalis Records sent the Fabulous Thunderbirds into the studio to record another album. Their previous three albums had been produced by their manager, Denny Bruce, but this time they wanted to use someone different.

They went up and down the list of possible producers several times before they agreed on the British-born Nick Lowe, who made a name for himself in the 1970s, first as the bassist for Dave Edmunds's band Rockpile, then later as a producer who had a major influence on the punk rock movement. In the late 1970s, he worked on projects with Elvis Costello, the Pretenders, and Graham Parker, to name a few.

The first time the T-Birds asked Lowe to produce their next album, he said no because he was too busy. But they kept asking until they caught him with downtime. For the Lowe-produced album, which they titled *T-Bird Rhythm*, they moved away from the horns and back to their original guitar sound, and they decided to record everything in their own backyard at Third Coast Studios in Austin.

Kim Wilson wrote only three songs for this album—"Can't Tear It Up Enuff," "Lover's Crime," and "Poor Boy"—but they were among the best songs they recorded for the session. "Can't Tear It Up Enuff" is a stop-start, 1950s-style rock 'n' roll number that was a forerunner of the song that would eventually give the band its greatest commercial success, "Tuff Enuff."

The other songs on the album provided a mixture of hard-core blues and hot-rod rock 'n' roll. On "Tell Me," a Jimmy Reed–style blues number, Kim really shines on both the vocal and harmonica. "Gotta Have Some/Just Got Some" offers a vocal that is reminiscent of Mose Allison, along with a guitar instead of a piano.

"Neighbor Tend to Your Business" is unique because of the hypnotic, dead-on groove that Fran and Keith slipped into for the duration of the song. On "You're Humbuggin' Me," Kim does outstanding harmonica work, proving that he is among the best in the business. With "How Do You Spell Love," a Memphis-style soul number, the T-Birds telegraphed a future direction for the band.

T-Bird Rhythm was a great album, with solid vocals and some of Jimmie's best guitar work to date, but the T-Bird's retro sound couldn't compete with the hit makers of 1982 for radio airtime. It was the year of Paul McCartney's and Stevie Wonder's "Ebony and Ivory" and Elton John's "Empty Garden," and there simply was no room on the charts for the type of music the T-Birds loved to play.

John Hammond was a wealthy New Yorker, an heir to the Vanderbilt fortune, who had an obsession for roots music, the civil rights movement, and the record business. As a record producer, he had worked with Bessie Smith, Fletcher Henderson, Pete Seeger, George Benson, and others. As a talent scout, he had discovered Aretha Franklin, Billie Holiday, Bob Dylan, and Bruce Springsteen.

When he received the tape that Stevie Ray Vaughan and Double Trouble recorded at Jackson Browne's studio, the fifty-one-year-old producer knew he had something special. His first instinct was to release the album on his own label, HME Records, which was distributed by CBS Records. But he feared that promotion would be too costly for him, and he played the tape for Gregg Geller, an executive at Epic Records, a subsidiary of CBS.

It was Geller's job to scout new talent, but he spent most of his time turning down starry-eyed substandard wannabes. When Hammond approached him with Stevie's tape, he figured he would find a way to let the music legend down gently—in the early 1980s, white boys playing the blues were not on anyone's A-list—but when he listened to the tape, he knew that Hammond was onto something.

Geller convinced his coworkers that Epic should release the album. One of his best arguments, aside from Stevie's obvious talent, was that the album had been recorded free of charge at Jackson Browne's studio, which meant that they did not have to advance money for production costs, only to the artist himself.

To Stevie's delight, he was offered $65,000 for the album, a pittance compared to what the label offered other major recording artists, but more money than Stevie and Double Trouble had ever seen before. No one complained or asked for more.

John Hammond was named executive producer, which meant that he received a fee to supervise the mixing of the album (the final step in the recording process, in which the sound levels of the various tracks on the tape are brought up or pushed down to achieve the most effective sound mix possible). That part of the process was stressful for Stevie because the much older Hammond was set in his ways and seemingly obsessed with small details that Stevie did not necessarily think were important.

Fortunately for all involved, Hammond did not think it was necessary for Stevie and the band to rerecord any portions of the album, which meant that they were on a fast track to becoming certified recording artists. The Fabulous Thunderbirds had released four albums, but none of them had generated advances as large as the one Stevie received and none of them had sold enough copies for the band members to make any money.

For Stevie and Double Trouble to make any money from the album beyond the advance, it would have to sell in excess of 130,000 copies (records sold for about $6 in those days and artists averaged royalties of about 8 percent), 100,000 more copies than the best-selling T-Bird album ever sold. No one but Stevie and the band considered that even a remote possibility.

The album was titled *Texas Flood*, after the track of the same name written by Larry Davis, a Little Rock–born bluesman who recorded on Duke Records in Texas. The blues ballad had been one of Stevie's favorite songs for a long time and he never gave a performance without including it on the song list. Stevie identified with the song so much that he was able to climb inside it and drive it anyplace he wanted.

The first song on the album, "Love Struck Baby," was the tune Stevie wrote on the day he moved in with Lenny. More old-time rock 'n' roll than blues, it had a driving beat and a guitar solo more reminiscent of rockabilly pioneer Carl Perkins than Jimi Hendrix. Stevie's vocal was rough but fit the music perfectly.

With "Pride and Joy," he slipped into more of a rhythm and blues groove, though the guitar solo still rocked, but with "Tell Me" he waded into a blues swamp and kept walking until he dropped clean out of sight, taking traditional blues notes and doubling, tripling, them into a unique creation of his own.

In "Testify," a high-octane instrumental, he used distortion techniques to lay down a pulsating rhythm at high amplification, then doubled back over that slippery hardwood floor to play his solo notes. It was that going back and forth that made him such an interesting guitarist to watch. It was sort of like tossing a ball, then running after it to catch it before it hit the ground. Nine times out of ten Stevie caught it.

"I'm Crying," an original composition, is important because it established Stevie as the master of the Texas shuffle, a rough-hewn mixture of rhythm and lead notes, enhanced by the extraordinarily thick strings he used on his guitar.

"Lenny" is a slow-temp instrumental Stevie wrote for his wife. When playing live, he sometimes liked to sit down on the stage and play it last, after the band had stood down and walked off the stage. In this song, he uses tremolo and vibrato techniques to lay down a foundation over which to play individual notes. It is a song that is filled with love, childlike wonderment and, at times, bafflement, all emotions he was feeling in his marriage at the time.

When *Texas Flood* was released in June 1983, John Hammond gave an interview to *Guitar World* and said, "The first great Texas guitar player I ever saw in the flesh was T-Bone Walker, back in 1936. And Stevie Ray is in that great tradition. He has such a direct quality. And he's a great showman, too, just like T-Bone was."

Before the year was over, *Texas Flood* peaked at number 38 on the Billboard album charts and sold more than half a million copies, a feat that astonished everyone, including Stevie, the band and his supporters at Epic Records. Not only would Epic recoup its initial investment of $65,000, it would be able to pay Stevie and the band an additional $235,000; at least that was the way it looked on the books.

Critically, the album was a big success. Stevie was nominated for two Grammy Awards: for "Texas Flood" in the Best Traditional Blues Recording category and for "Rude Mood" in the Best Rock Instrumental category. In addition, he won in three categories in *Guitar Player* magazine readers' poll: Best Blues Guitarist, in which he beat out Eric Clapton, along with Best New Talent and Best Blues Album.

Once the album went into production and distribution, Stevie and the band hit the road. In Texas, they appeared on *Austin City Limits,* the popular television show carried by public stations across the country, and they performed on the East Coast in a variety of venues. All the while, Stevie's alcohol and drug habit escalated to the point where those around him began to fear for his health and safety. Drugs were literally tossed his way from every direction by people who wanted to curry favor with him.

Aside from landing the record deal, the biggest event of 1983 occurred in early December, when Stevie went to Hamilton, Ontario, to perform on an hour-long television show with one of his heroes, Albert King. The show, named *In Session*, was one of several produced by Ian Anderson. The idea was to pair artists who were musically similar but hadn't recorded together. Other shows paired B. B. King with Larry Carlton, and Dr. John with Johnny Winter.

Albert King wasn't sure who Stevie Ray Vaughan was, but he agreed to do the show anyway. Those involved in the production were a little anxious because the bluesman had a reputation for being hard to get along with. Rough on the exterior *and* the interior, the sixty-year-old guitarist was hard-core blues, which meant that he didn't put much store in social niceties or fancy talk.

Stax Records, the Memphis-based label that brought him so much success in the early 1970s, folded in 1975 and the past few years had been rough on King. Illiterate and often abused by the industry, he had to fight hard for everything he got and had a reputation for being hard to work with.

Don Nix, the Stax staffer who produced and wrote most of King's acclaimed *Lovejoy* album, said that the guitarist could be difficult to work with at times, but mainly just wanted to get the job done so that he could leave the studio and go home.

Typically, for King's sessions there was not a lot of discussion about how to make the record. "I would get a line, a guitar line—back then they all had one that they repeated—and you just write a song on top of it," Nix explained. "When you get that down, you start putting things on top of it. I'd just show the players a couple of simple lines." Nix said that King never complained about the system.

"Albert was an artist," said Nix. "'Just show me what to do. Show me where to stand. Tell me what you want me to do.' He had done that stuff for so long, his attitude was, Get me in, get me out."

That was the attitude that King carried to the television studio in Hamilton. He had no "vision" for how the program should be conducted and he really didn't care who was going to be on the show with him. He just wanted to know where the director wanted him to stand and what they wanted him to play. *Get me in, get me out!* That's all he asked of those around him.

King couldn't place Stevie's name at first but when Stevie walked in the door, King recognized him instantly as the skinny white kid who had played guitar on stage with him in Austin. That was cool with King.

Nearly two hours of music were taped for the sixty-minute show, during which King and Stevie interacted for the cameras, with the younger guitarist showing deference to the master, despite having an album out that was outselling all of King's albums combined.

They played a mixture of songs recorded by both Stevie and King, though the decided edge went to the older guitarist. Two of the songs, "Ask Me No Questions" and "Match Box Blues," were on King's current album. Stevie contributed "Pride and Joy" from his current album.

On "Call It Stormy Monday," the blues ballad written by T-Bone Walker that Bobby "Blue" Bland had a big hit with in the 1960s, they traded guitar riffs, with King doing the vocal. Afterward they talked for the cameras.

"I remember the first time I met you," said Stevie, then he told about the first time he heard King play in Austin.

"Yeah," King said, laughing. "You were standing around there looking, and I said, who is that little skinny thing . . . then the night you sat in with us, I was listening but you thought I wasn't, but I was listening. I thought about it all the way back to Illinois and I said, he's got the makings of a good fiddler . . . well, sure enough . . . that's what you get for paying attention."

Then they went into "Pride and Joy," with King alternating with Stevie, playing rhythm and sometimes shouting with joy over the music. The rhythm section, composed of Gus Thornton on bass and Michael Llorens on drums, wasn't Double Trouble, but it stayed tight with the guitar wizards, though sometimes not pushing hard enough.

During the lunch break, King went around to the staff members asking if anyone had an emery board. Stevie saw him doing that, but he didn't think anything about it. Later, Stevie told Dan Forte about it in a conversation that was repeated in the liner notes of the *In Session* CD released in 1999 by Fantasy Records.

Recalled Stevie: "We were jamming on the last song, and it comes to the solo, and [King] goes, 'Get it, Stevie!' I started off, and I look over and he's pulling out this damn emery board, filing his nails, sort of giving me this sidelong glace. I loved it! Lookin' at me like, 'Uh-huh. I got you swinging from your toes.'"

Toward the end of the show, King told Stevie that although he was good, he was going to get even better. The trick, he explained, was to never stop trying. Stevie promised he would never stop trying and King said he would be praying for him.

Perhaps because it was a Canadian show, syndicated only north of the border, it never received the attention it should have in the States. It is a stark reminder not only of the debt that Stevie owed to bluesmen such as Albert King, but of the breadth of the cultural divide that separated the two men.

The following month, King went to Berkeley, California, to record what would become his last album, *I'm in a Phone Booth, Baby*, and Stevie went to New York's Power Station Studios to record his second album, *Couldn't Stand the Weather*. John Hammond was asked to be the producer. Listed as the executive producer on the previous album, he had merely supervised the mixing and mastering of the tapes. This time he was asked for guidance at every step of the way, although he ended up being more of an inspiration for Stevie than a hands-on producer. Stevie was the album's actual producer.

Eight songs made it onto the album, four of them written by Stevie. The standout track on the album is probably Stevie's "Couldn't Stand the Weather," a stop-start throwback to the early jazz songs of the 1920s that used silence as just another instrument. Of course, there was nothing jazzy about the song—it rocked from start to finish. So he wouldn't have to play rhythm and then overdub his solos, he asked Jimmie to come to New York to play second guitar.

"['Couldn't Stand the Weather'] started out being about not getting along with the wife, then I started to see that it had more to do than with just my little world," Stevie later explained. "It had to do with a lot of other things and I tried to just express it."

Although Stevie and Jimmie had played together often, it was the first time they ever recorded in a studio together. The results were spectacular. Jimmie was also asked to play on a second song, "The Things (That) I Used to Do," a torch ballad of the type played every Saturday night in dives all up and down the Mississippi Delta. Stevie's vocal was soulful to the extreme, but it was the wicked, to-hell-and-back guitar work that energized the song.

T-Bird drummer Fran Christina also was asked to play on one of the album's tracks, "Stang's Swang." It was a jazz instrumental that called for high-powered finesse on the snare—and Christina delivered perfectly. The song was recorded in one take.

A second instrumental Stevie took credit for writing, "Scuttle Buttin'," also dazzled, but its appeal was dimmed somewhat by the fact that the song is almost identical to a song titled "Hold It," written by Clifford Scott and Billy Butler. The song was recorded by Stax Record's house band, the Mar-Keys, in the 1960s and went on to become a staple intermission song for bands all across the South.

In February, a month after the session wrapped, Stevie attended the Grammy Awards, where he won in the Best Traditional Blues Recording category for his performance of "Texas Flood" on *Blues Explosion*, an album that Atlantic Records had put out featuring some of the artists at the Montreux festival.

Couldn't Stand the Weather was released in May 1984 to critical acclaim and went on to sell more than a million copies and earn Stevie a Grammy nomination in the Best Rock Instrumental category for "Voodoo Chile," a Jimi Hendrix song that acknowledged Stevie's indebtedness to one of his childhood heroes.

Stevie's first professional publicist, Charles Comer, went into overdrive, pitching "his Stevie," as he referred to him, to newspapers and magazine across the country. A former publicist for the Beatles and the Rolling Stones, he knew all the angles, which meant that Stevie and his music would get coverage in publications that had not written about the blues in years, if ever. He had as much to do with Stevie's future success as anyone. No one becomes a star based on radio play alone. Comer understood that better than anyone in the business and he made sure that "his Stevie" was known to every writer in America and beyond.

As Stevie's career took off with meteoric suddenness, the Fabulous Thunderbirds seemed to flounder. The band had released four albums, none of which had sold more than 50,000 copies, while Stevie was selling nearly 3,000 copies a day of his records. It's one thing to view the success of others from a distance, but when it is someone you know, someone you have worked with in the trenches, that success takes on very personal characteristics.

The T-Birds had always been prone to take out their frustrations on each other, but as Stevie's star shined brighter and brighter with each passing day, the band members seemed to quarrel more often. Jimmie and Kim often got into fistfights, but no one thought much about that because they always laughed it off and got back to business. When Kim and bass player Keith Ferguson started duking it out, well, that was a different story. Keith was an important member of the T-Birds, but he was not the most important.

By August 1984, both Jimmie and Kim had had enough.

"Roomful and the T-Birds were very close, for years—and Jimmie and I had talked about playing together and me joining the band a few times, but nothing came of it," then Roomful of Blues bassist Preston Hubbard recalled. "Then Jimmie called me up and said, 'Let's do it.' We picked the same afternoon when I would give Roomful notice and for him to talk to Keith."

Jimmie told Keith that they were dropping him from the band. "They wanted somebody else," Keith told the *Dallas Observer*. "That's what [Jimmie] told me. Just wanted to do something new. So I went looking for other work."

"Keith was really a dear friend of theirs, Jimmie especially—and Roomful was my family," said Preston. "When I called the Roomful guys together to tell them, John Roxy, our drummer, already knew. So there was a pipeline between Providence and Austin that was faster than the Internet."

Preston recalls first meeting the T-Birds in 1976. "We worked with Buddy [Guy] a lot in the Northeast and he was at the Original Antone's and he told us about this band out of Texas," says Preston. "He said, 'Man, you've got to hear these guys out of Texas, the Thunderbirds,' and he had told them about us. Finally, we met one night in Boston for the first time. It was like an instant bond. Then we started doing a lot of gigs together. We'd bring them up into the Northeast, because Roomful was well known there and they brought us to Texas for the first time and they were already huge in Texas. That was when I first met Stevie, Lou Ann, the Cobras, that whole crew."

Leaving Roomful wasn't easy for Preston, but he was ready for a new adventure. Actually, it was probably more of an adventure than he bargained for. By that point, Jimmie and Keith Ferguson were the only two T-Birds who were born in Texas. With Keith's departure and Preston's arrival, that meant that Jimmie was the only non-Yankee in the group, not a distinction that automatically made the band new friends.

"I stepped into a huge controversy," says Preston. "It was amazing! It blew my mind. It was in the press and people had formed up and taken sides—the Keith people and the Thunderbirds/Preston people. It was really weird. At first there were people close to the band who would barely speak to me. I had to prove myself. Keith was one in a million. The first gig was great. We didn't even rehearse. We'd known each other so long, I knew their stuff. We did gigs in Waco; it was all Texas stuff."

After obtaining a new manager, Mark Proct (a T-Bird roadie who worked his way up into a management position), the T-Birds set out on a national and European tour. They didn't have much choice. The band was more than $175,000 in debt, according to Preston, and they were desperate for money.

"We hit the road in clubs all over the States," Preston wrote in his unpublished autobiography, "Into the Abyss." "The T-Birds were still pretty much cult status at the time, despite the four incredible records that were already out, but our crowds were fanatical, here and in Europe. I managed to stay fairly heroin-free in those early days, but not by my own design. I mostly didn't have any connects except in certain big cities and back home in Austin. But there was plenty of booze, courtesy of our [contract] rider, and lots of coke. Lots and lots of coke. And we did it all, took all offers . . . and , of course, there were girls. Hundreds of girls. Nameless, faceless one-nighters, gone forever from my memory. Some remain with me, though I couldn't tell you their names if my life depended on it, and a few became actual road girlfriends who I stayed in touch with and saw once a year or so (even if they had married in the interim), but most have faded into the obscurity that comes with time and copious amounts of booze and drugs."

For Stevie Ray Vaughan, Memphis was the apex of the music universe, the place where all the passions, sweet harmonies, and exotic rhythms of his life converged. Texas was his birthplace, where he learned to walk, talk, and play guitar, but Memphis was his soul place, where he could sidle up to the mysterious power of the universe—and, if he was lucky on that particular day, reach out and caress it.

Memphis is the birthplace of the blues, where at the turn of the twentieth century, W. C. Handy gathered up the African American folk rhythms of the Mississippi Delta, blended them with classical European instrumentation, and created what we now call the blues by casting them like rolling dice on the gritty cobblestones of Beale Street.

A half century later, Memphis is where Scotty Moore, Bill Black, and Elvis Presley sauntered into a Union Avenue recording studio named Memphis Recording Service on a hot July night and conjured a new music that others subsequently named rock 'n' roll.

Blues and rock 'n' roll were two beats in the same artery, and no one understood that better than Stevie Ray Vaughan, which was why Memphis excited him and frightened him at the same instant, for there was always the question in the back of his mind: What if Memphis doesn't take to me?

He didn't know that Memphis takes to anything raw. That's how it's always been. When the city first took in the blues, it was in pretty rough shape. Over a period of decades, African American folk music slowly developed from crude rhymes and chants to a type of single chord music that was more notable for rhythm and passion than melodic construction. Early musicians typically sang to the accompaniment of a single chord of music, moving their voices up and down the harmonic scale as the music marched in place contributing little to the song except a beat.

In 1912 Handy set African American folk music free to grow and prosper during the 1920s and 1930s as the blues; radio allowed the music to reach a mass audience. Three radio stations—WDIA in Memphis, WLAC in Nashville, and KFFA in Helena, Arkansas—propelled the blues into the mainstream of American life.

By the 1940s, white southerners had a knowledge of the blues, usually in a refined form that had been sifted and diluted at recording studios in New York. But access to live music was limited by the social restrictions of the time. There was no socially acceptable way of listening to the blues. Radio, the first truly democratic music venue, made the blues accessible to everyone.

In fact B. B. King started his career in 1949 as a disc jockey at WDIA. He used his popularity at the radio station to land a record deal for "Three O'Clock Blues," a song released in 1950 that made the national rhythm and blues charts. After that, King recorded anywhere and everywhere that he could. "We went to homes, the YMCA, wherever [they] could find me," King said. "They would set up portable equipment and put blankets against the wall to make it sound better."

As King was making a name for himself, Chess Records recruited Ike Turner as a talent scout to find blues artists for its roster. His first big find was Howlin' Wolf, a West Memphis radio deejay he recorded on portable equipment in 1948.

Listening to B. B. King and Howlin' Wolf on radio was Sam Phillips, an employee at radio station WREC, which catered to a white audience. He was so impressed by what he heard that he quit his job and set up his own recording studio, which he named Memphis Recording Service. King was one of his first customers. Recalled King: "The company I worked for made a deal with Phillips's studio that anything I wanted to record—and they had the time to do—they would let me do."

Phillips also recorded Howlin' Wolf, Ike Turner, Walter Horton, Joe Hill Louis, and others. Some of his recordings he sold to record labels in Los Angeles and Chicago; others he released on his own label, Sun Records.

After doing that for a couple of years, Phillips realized that building a record label around black artists was a risky business. In the 1950s, it was illegal for blacks to mingle with whites. Blacks could be arrested if they entered hotels, restaurants, or even the public library. Phillips took a lot of heat for spending so much time with black artists, heat he was willing to take, rebel that he was; but problems soon arose when labels outside the South started competing for his artists, luring them to Chicago. Howlin' Wolf was one of the artists who abandoned Phillips and went north. Soon there was a virtual stampede—and who could blame them? The Memphis racial climate was abrasive and volatile.

As much as he loved rhythm and blues, Phillips had to face reality: The records sold, but not well enough to ever make it onto the pop charts, where the real money was. When he held that up against the racial politics of recording and marketing blues, and the lack of loyalty the artists showed toward him, it became clear that his fledgling record label was headed for hard times. What he really needed was a white artist who could make it onto the pop charts. It was at that point in his life, that Elvis Presley, Scotty Moore, and Bill Black walked into the studio in 1954, eager to make a record.

At that time, the chart toppers were Doris Day's "Secret Love," Frank Sinatra's "Young at Heart," and Perry Como's "Idle Gossip." There wasn't a chance in hell that any of the rhythm and blues records that Phillips released would ever make it into that lily-white league. With Elvis, Scotty, and Bill—they named themselves the Blue Moon Boys—Phillips saw an opportunity to tiptoe into the Big Time.

By breathing life into rock 'n' roll, the Blue Moon Boys did exactly that. Although it took two years for Elvis's records to make it into the Top 20 on the pop charts, his success opened the door for Phillips to sign new talent and make Sun Records the label of choice for emerging rock 'n' roll talent. Before the 1950s were over, Philips discovered an amazing roster of talent, including Jerry Lee Lewis, Carl Perkins, Johnny Cash, Roy Orbison, and many others.

Going into the 1960s, Memphis *owned* rock 'n' roll. Different strains of the music popped up in New York, Philadelphia, St. Louis, and New Orleans, but there was no question in anyone's mind about where the music originated.

Watching the success of Sun Records from across town was Jim Stewart and his sister, Estelle Axton. They pooled their resources—he worked in the bond department of a Memphis bank and she worked as a bookkeeper—and started up their own record company, which they named Satellite Productions (Russia's Sputnik had made satellite a household word). After renting a vacant movie theater for $100 a month to house their recording equipment, they renamed the company Stax Records (a combination of Stewart and Axton).

Their first hit was in 1961 with "Gee Whiz," sung by teenager Carla Thomas. "It took me a while to see the significance of what I was getting into," Thomas later recalled. "What I thought was fun was a business. Being young, black, and in the sixties, it was a thrill to just record."

Stax followed that up the same year with "Last Night," an instrumental recorded by the Mar-Keys, a group that later formed the nucleus of the record label's house band. The following year, they added a black organist and drummer to the house band, forming a group called Booker T. and the MGs, which had a hit in 1962 titled "Green Onions."

What made Stax unique in those days was its permissive racial attitude. Although it was illegal in Memphis for whites and blacks to gather in public places, Jim and Estelle encouraged black and white musicians to work together in their studio. Booker T. and the MGs was a racially mixed band, a real rarity in American music at that time.

People forget, but soul music did not originate at a grassroots level. No one ever played it on street corners in Memphis, the way they did the blues. Sweet soul music did not migrate up Highway 61 to Memphis from Mississippi; it was created inside a single studio through the vision of Jim and Estelle.

Stax's success was based on two principles, one of them musical and the other social. Horns had been used on recordings since the first jazz sessions, but no one ever thought to use horns to replace a human chorus. The first mark of Stewart's genius was his decision to use horns, typically just a trumpet and a saxophone, in those places on a record where listeners were accustomed to hearing human choruses. The results were dazzling. The second mark of his genius was to engage in what amounted to social experimentation.

What would happen, Stewart wondered, if black musicians were placed in a room with white musicians, not to play old music but to invent new sounds. The result was the "sweet soul" music that made Stax recording artists international sensations. Booker T. and the MGs, Sam and Dave, Otis Redding, Albert King, Isaac Hayes, the Staple Singers, Rufus Thomas, Carla Thomas, and others were the faces and voices associated with the music, but the geniuses behind it all were Jim Stewart and Estelle Axton.

As Stax was tearing up the charts with its soul-based music in the 1960s, two additional Memphis recording studios rose to national prominence—Willie Mitchell's Hi Records and Chips Moman's American Recording Studio. In the mid-1960s and beyond, Mitchell produced a series of hit records, working with Ann Peebles, Tina Turner, and his biggest discovery of all, Al Green.

American Recording Studio's first hit was an up-tempo rock song, "Keep On Dancing," recorded by a group of white Memphis teenagers who called themselves the Gentrys. It was followed by Sandy Posey's "Born a Woman," and then later by the first number 1 record ever to come out of Memphis, "The Letter," by the Box Tops.

"I wouldn't turn anything down," Moman later recalled. "There was a ten-year period in which I might have averaged three hours of sleep a night. I recorded one time for nine days without going home. I would fall unconscious behind the board and people would pick me up and shake me and say, 'Can you do one more mix?'—when they should have taken me straight to a hospital."

From 1968, when Moman produced Elvis Presley's heralded hits "In the Ghetto," "Suspicious Minds," and "Kentucky Rain," until 1971, the studio turned out eighty-three singles and twenty-five albums that made the national charts. Among them were two albums from Neil Diamond, *Brother Love* and *Touching You*, which contained the hit singles "Sweet Caroline" and "Holly Holy"; Dusty Springfield's "Son of a Preacher Man" and "Windmills of Your Mind"; Joe Tex's "Hold On to What You Got"; Petula Clark's "People Get Ready"; and Dionne Warwick's "Lost That Lovin' Feeling."

For a time, Memphis was at the center of America's musical universe. It started falling apart in 1973, when Chips Moman abruptly moved to Nashville because he couldn't stand the Memphis musicians' bickering. His departure was followed in 1975 by the closing of Stax Records. One year later, Al Green gave up his recording career to become a minister, leaving Willie Mitchell without a star.

Estelle Axton and Bobby Manuel, a former Stax producer, had the last word in 1976, when they released Rick Dees's "Disco Duck" and watched it soar to the number 1 position on the national charts. Manuel reveled in the success of the record, but he had known that the music scene in Memphis was stone-cold dead the year before, when he and Jim Stewart went to the bankruptcy sale for the equipment that had been in the Stax studio. "To see people sitting in the courtroom cutting cocaine and laughing, taking hits in the courtroom—I will never forget it," says Manuel. "They were like wolves." Manuel and Stewart left the courthouse empty-handed after one buyer purchased the entire lot of equipment for $50,000.

Seven decades of Memphis music ended with the pounding of a judicial gavel, amid hushed, desperate voices and the white, powdery stain of cocaine.

By the time Stevie Ray Vaughan made his first trip to Memphis in June 1984, he was nearly quaking in his boots. He was in awe of the city and the many recording artists who had called the city their home. Booked at an annual music festival called MusicFest, Stevie and Double Trouble performed with dozens of other blues and rock acts. Those who remember seeing Stevie then say he had tombstone eyes from the deadly mixture of cocaine and whisky that flowed through his body.

Sadly, at the time of Stevie's first visit to Memphis, the city was a musical wasteland. A number 1 single had not been recorded there since Rick Dees's "Disco Duck." There were only a handful of recording studios left, Ardent Recording being the most successful. Beale Street looked like a war zone, with boarded up buildings, no nightclubs, and only one business in operation. Memphis music was like a corpse laid out in a pine box—you could look at it, you could remark on what a good life it had lived, but you couldn't talk to it.

Stevie left Memphis without ever tapping into the city's musical legacy. It turned out to be just another gig. It might as well have been Baltimore or Cedar Rapids. Despite the success of two albums, he didn't think anyone had noticed him perform that day. He was wrong about that. Watching him were the booking agent for the Orpheum, Memphis's historic theater, and members of the Blues Foundation, which three years earlier had begun giving out awards known as "Handys" (named after W. C. Handy).

Stevie and Double Trouble were invited back to Memphis in September to perform at the Orpheum with headliner Koko Taylor, who began her career in Memphis and later found success in Chicago, where she was often billed as the Queen of Chicago Blues, a label that she sometimes found disagreeable.

Music writer Brown Burnett did a preconcert interview with Taylor in which she acknowledged Stevie Ray Vaughan as the "new kid on the block" but focused on Taylor and what Burnett saw as a decline in the public's appreciation of the blues.

"You know, the blues doesn't get airplay on the radio any more, so it's not easy keeping it alive," Taylor said. "I'm firmly convinced that if the black people won't keep it alive, the white people will. It will survive."

Stevie was among the "white people" who were doing just that, and his dedication was not lost on the Koko Taylors of the world or the Blues Foundation, which was compiling its list of winners for its next awards show in November.

A little over two weeks after his performance at the Orpheum, Stevie went to New York City to celebrate his thirtieth birthday and gave one of the most important concerts of his career. Since John Hammond had held his first Spirituals to Swing concert at Carnegie Hall in 1939, blues performers had been a rarity at New York's premier concert venue. When Stevie was asked to perform on October 4, 1984, he knew the importance of the booking. He was the new voice of the blues; it was up to him to carry the torch into the cool darkness of New York's high society.

Joining Stevie and Double Trouble at the concert were Jimmie Vaughan, New Orleans's Dr. John, Antone's house band, Austin blues singer Angela Strehli, and the Roomful of Blues horn section. Everyone rehearsed in Texas for a week before going to New York, then ran through the program at Carnegie Hall on the afternoon of the performance.

With Martha and Big Jim Vaughan in the audience, Stevie took the stage that evening determined to bring the house down. It didn't go exactly that way. The big band he had assembled for the occasion was loose and disjointed, performing with only a fraction of the tightness usually displayed by the trio.

For the first few songs, the audience was shockingly reserved. Everyone clapped politely, but no one stood up and cheered. Desperate, he broke into the one song that always worked in concert, Jimi

Hendrix's "Voodoo Chile." When the song ended, he was astonished that everyone was still seated. Seeing his hero's pain, a T-shirt clad member of the audience rose to his feet and shouted, "Stand up! This ain't *La Traviata!*"

That's all that was needed, for some Texas swamp rabbit to hop through the diamond-and-fur set to spark a stampede—and it did! Luckily, the audience clapped and sometimes rose to their feet instead of making a desperate dash for the door as Stevie's heavy-metal blues shook the crystal chandeliers in the lobby with hurricane force.

For the remainder of the evening, the captive audience behaved more like a concert crowd than an operatic one, leading reviewers to pronounce the concert an outstanding success. The *New York Times* compared the normally staid venue with a roadhouse, and *Newsday* compared Stevie to B. B. King.

When Stevie saw Martha and Big Jim after the concert, both parents had tears streaming down their cheeks. Never in their wildest dreams had they expected Stevie to outshine Jimmie. To see their two sons on the most important stage in the country filled them with pride. There was a downside, however. Big Jim was in a wheelchair, battling Parkinson's disease. He would not be long for this world.

Not long after leaving New York, Stevie and the band flew to Japan, where they gave an electrifying performance in Tokyo—and then it was on to Australia, where they performed in Melbourne, Adelaide, and Brisbane, and then gave three sold-out performances at the Sydney Opera House.

While they were in Australia, Stevie received word that he had won two Handy Awards: Entertainer of the Year and Blues Instrumentalist of the Year. The previous year, Clarence "Gatemouth" Brown had won the Entertainer of the Year Award and Albert Collins had won Blues Instrumentalist of the Year. Stevie was the only white performer to ever win awards in those categories.

Five days after his final performance at the Sydney Opera House, he was in Memphis for the third time that year, to attend the fifth annual National Blues Awards sponsored by the Blues Foundation, a Memphis-based nonprofit organization dedicated to the preservation and perpetuation of the blues.

Stevie was elated to be back in Memphis for the ceremony, which was held at the Orpheum. Joining him on stage was his friend Albert King, along with a host of other blues luminaries. Stevie was almost speechless. Memphis was honoring *him*. He played the blues, but Memphis *was* the blues!

At the conclusion of the ceremony, Stevie participated in an all-star jam as everyone joined in on B. B. King's classic, "Every Day I Have the Blues." Whether it was because of cocaine or his own humility at being in the same room with so many people who had performed with Howlin' Wolf, Muddy Waters, and Jimmy Reed, Stevie kept his head bowed the entire evening. On the final jam, he watched his fingers caress and pick at the strings of his guitar, expressing a childlike awe at the sound that emerged. For blues musicians, Memphis is the Promised Land—and Stevie, at that moment, knew that he had arrived at the gates and found them opened wide.

In March 1985, Stevie and Double Trouble went into Dallas Sound Labs studio in Dallas to record a new album titled *Soul to Soul*. Several weeks before that, Stevie and Jimmie went to the funeral of a mutual friend, someone who had died at an early age of a heart attack brought on by cocaine use. It rattled Stevie to see his friend laid out in a coffin, but the shock was not powerful enough to dissuade him from ingesting massive amounts of cocaine and whisky, usually mixed in a potent cocktail that he began drinking in the morning and continued downing all through the day and into the night.

Stevie was a hard-core addict, but he wouldn't listen to anyone who suggested that he pull back—and it affected his music in ways that he was too stoned to understand. He didn't have a plan when he went into the studio; he just wanted to record an album and he figured everything would fall into place.

Prior to beginning the session, Stevie tried to get in touch with Reese Wynans, a veteran keyboard man who had played with Delbert McClinton and Jerry Jeff Walker, but every time he got a telephone number for Reese and called it, he was told that the number had been disconnected. He desperately wanted to offer Reese a permanent position with the band. As their recordings became more and more ambitious, it became obvious to him that the band needed a stronger rhythm section. Stevie was finding it increasingly difficult to play both rhythm and lead guitar, especially after lengthy cocaine jags. He didn't want another guitarist in the band, so adding a keyboard player seemed the best solution.

Stevie and the band were already at work on the album when Reese strolled into the studio and said he understood that Stevie was looking for him. Reese readily accepted Stevie's offer to join the band and asked when he wanted him to start.

"Today," said Stevie.

Unlike the recording they had done at Jackson Browne's studio and Power Station in New York, where they had played in relative isolation, they set up the Dallas studio so that they could record live, simulating the setup they used on stage. When everyone is playing at once, it is more difficult to balance the individual instruments, but Stevie wanted to do it that way because he felt that it would help them record a better album.

"We're recording the old way and using the best modern equipment we can find—it's a good combination," Stevie told Bruce Nixon, a *Guitar World* writer who went to Dallas while the band was still in the studio. "We go in and cut a song a few times if we need to, or just do a set. At this point, we're pretty fine-tuned, and we're watching it grow as it goes. We're all examining everything. We have a lot of ideas, things we've wanted to have a chance to work with."

Stevie didn't take any original songs to the session, just made them up while he and the band rehearsed in the studio. Typically they arrived in the studio at 10:00 p.m. and worked through the night, wrapping at around 6:00 a.m.

Stevie sometimes heard music in his head that he couldn't explain to the other band members. That happened with "Empty Arms," a Stevie original that they had recorded for the previous album and then cut from the lineup. Stevie wanted to record it again for their new album, but he couldn't explain what he was hearing for the drum part, so he sat down and played it himself.

"One day he went in; I don't remember if it was in the middle of the night or something," Chris Layton told Craig Lee Hopkins. "They were in the studio and he sat down at the drums and had [the engineer] record he and Tommy doing the whole song, and then he went back and put the guitars on top of it. He knew just the right speed and exactly the way it needed to feel. It was a weird kind of feel—we call it the 'backwards shuffle.'"

Soul to Soul ended up with five songs written by Stevie and three written by his old friend Doyle Bramhall. In addition to Reese on keyboards, they added a saxophone to get a more uptown, soulful sound.

The most memorable song on the album is probably Stevie's "Ain't Gone 'n' Give Up on Love," a soulful ballad about struggling with love. Reese was exceptional on organ and Stevie's guitar riff dripped with emotion. "It's actually an answer to a Larry Davis song that was not recorded," Stevie later explained. "It was a song that he was writing for me. I think it was, 'I Will Give Up on Love Before Love Gives Up on Me.'"

"He submitted it to me and I said, 'Hey this doesn't sound like something I would say. I want to turn it around.' I did. I was hoping that by putting that on the sleeve of the record that it would help him get a deal. At the time, he didn't have a deal. He's a great writer, a great musician, a great singer. He's the writer for 'Texas Flood,' 'As Years Go Passing By,' and many great blues songs. I want to do some more work with him."

"Say What," the lead track on the album, was another one of Stevie's instrumental compositions. It offered one of his patented Texas shuffles, with lots of distortion and rocketing high notes that blended well with Reese's surprisingly derivative "Hot Pastrami" organ part.

"Gone Home," the second instrumental on the album, showed off Reese's considerable skill as a jazz organist and allowed Stevie to slow down to do the sort of delicate fingering that he was so good at when he allowed himself the chance. Stevie and Reese literally talked to each other through their instruments all the way through the song, creating a conversation that was at times oddly poetic. Many people consider it the best track on the album.

While they were making the album, Stevie took a day off to travel to Austin to play an outdoor concert with the Fabulous Thunderbirds at the Manor Downs in Austin. "This particular show found Stevie and friends a little too high in front of 10,000 friends," wrote Keri Leigh in *Stevie Ray: Soul to Soul*. "Stevie merely went through the motions on 'Voodoo Chile,' playing the same old lines, making no attempt to step outside the safe zone. He looked tired, and rather than going to the trouble to dress up in his usual flamboyant stagewear, he dressed in a simple pair of Levi's and a sweatshirt, topped by a Mexican poncho to keep him warm on the chilly winter night. Stevie was more than a little tipsy—he'd been hitting the juice all day."

Even within the ragged perimeter of Stevie's dazed performance, there was joy in seeing the Vaughan brothers reunited on stage. For T-Bird bassist Fran Christina, it was always a thrill to watch the brothers perform together. "Jimmie would come up behind Stevie's back with a double neck guitar and he would play the rhythm and Stevie the lead, and then they would switch," says Fran. "It was like one was the extension of the other."

For the first time in a long time, the brothers knew the closeness they had felt when they were very young. Although Stevie was more successful at that point, he made an effort to include his brother whenever possible and he told interviewers that Jimmie was the best guitarist in the family. Jimmie didn't view Stevie's generosity as charity but as a visible sign of the bond that existed between them.

Stevie took another a day off from working on the album to perform on the opening-day game at the Houston Astrodome. Baseball legend Mickey Mantle was there to throw out the first ball. Everyone was feeling all warm and fuzzy. Then during the pregame festivities, Stevie strolled out into centerfield and played Jim Hendrix's version of "The Star Spangled Banner." It was a supreme misjudgment on Stevie's part and the crowd reacted predictably by booing him and throwing objects at him.

Of course, there was more to Stevie's questionable judgment and outrageous intake of cocaine and alcohol that met the eye. His marriage to Lenny was falling apart and Stevie had a difficult time grappling with that. His thinking was screwed up from drugs and alcohol and he felt no one could understand him. He became difficult to be around and created one nightmare after another for his publicist Charles Comer, as he was short with interviewers and sometimes exploded with pointless obscenities and nonsensical temper tantrums.

When *Soul to Soul* was released, some critics panned it, saying that it didn't have the fire evident in the previous two albums. *Rolling*

Stone magazine suggested that perhaps the band had "run out of gas." The album peaked at number 34 on the charts, but it eventually turned gold, signifying sales of 500,000.

Ordinarily that would be cause for celebration, but since the previous album had sold over a million copies, some critics suggested that the band had reached a plateau from which it would be difficult to move higher.

If you consider that when the album was released, the artists really tearing up the charts were Phil Collins ("Don't Lose My Number"), Madonna ("Dress You Up"), and Whitney Houston ("Saving All My Love for You"), it is easy to see why some critics were pessimistic about the future of blues-rock.

Blues had been a hard sell on the pop charts ever since the arrival of the rock era. Stevie had done better than anyone could have guessed with his blend of hard rock and blues, but by 1985 music critics were pretty much of the opinion that Stevie had finished his run as a hit maker. They wondered why Stevie didn't understand that.

From the album's debut in October 1985 to the end of the year, Stevie was on the road to promote it, teaming up with the Fabulous Thunderbirds for more than fifty one-nighters. Stevie was in bad shape by that time.

Sometimes he swayed off-rhythm while he played, rocking back and forth, terrorizing the backstage crew, who were fearful that he was going to fall flat on his face in the middle of a song. To "help" him out, they sent out a constant stream of cocaine-spiked whiskeys, just enough juice, they thought, to keep him going. Jimmie was having problems of his own, so he was in no position to help Stevie slam on the brakes. As a result, Stevie slipped deeper and deeper in the abyss.

In November 1985, Stevie was notified that he had won another Handy Award in the blues instrumentalist category, but he was unable to attend because he was out on the road promoting *Soul to Soul*.

Robert Cray, Koko Taylor, and John Lee Hooker were the big winners that year in a program that featured B. B. King and Willie Nelson as cohosts. When introducing Nelson that night, King said, "Most people would not associate him with the blues. He's a handsome young guy with long hair, and he's been playing country music, but he wrote my theme song, 'Nightlife.'" Nelson told the audience that the blues had been instrumental in his life. Later he confessed to a reporter that he had a burning desire to record a blues album of his own.

By that point, King was the unofficial host of the annual awards show. "I've always thought of Memphis as being the home of the blues—not Chicago, not the other places," he explained, pointing out that the Handy Awards are important because of the attention they focus on the blues.

"There are a lot of people who don't pay much attention to the blues as a whole, but the prestige of the awards makes people stop and think, particularly people in the movies and television," King said. "When Robert Cray won, his name was mentioned much more than it had been before. It was the same way with Stevie Ray Vaughan, even though he was a star before. It gives them the recognition of people who are in the blues field and know the blues."

CHAPTER 4

Is It *Tuff Enuff* for You, Stevie?

IT HAD BEEN three years since the Fabulous Thunderbirds released an album, and individual members of the band were demoralized. Stevie and Double Trouble were selling records by the truckload, proving that there was a market for Texas-style blues and rock 'n' roll, so what, exactly, was the problem, they wondered?

"We had been trying to get a record deal for months and months," recalled Fran Christina. "We had been turned down by several labels, two, three, four times apiece."

Finally, with the help of their new manager, Mark Proct, they landed a deal with a small label, which, to this day, they refuse to utter the name of. With four albums that did not sell, they knew this would probably be their last shot at fame and fortune, so they called the producer they felt would present them in the best light, British roots rocker Dave Edmunds, with whom they had built a friendship.

"It was just a matter of making it worthwhile for him to come in on the project," said Kim Wilson. "Money is essential. If you have nothing to offer, there's no sense in calling people."

Before leaving Austin, they rehearsed at Antone's during the day, going over the songs they thought would be good for the album. In the spring of 1985, with a label, a producer, and some advance money lined up, the T-Birds set out for London, where Edmunds wanted to record the album at a favorite place, Maison Rouge Studios. They rented two apartments near the studio and prepared to record what they realized would be either the best album of their career or the last.

On the flight over, Kim wrote down the lyrics for a new song on a barf bag, but he didn't tell anyone about it right away. He also took a song with him that he had culled from a ten-song sampler sent to him by a Memphis publishing company. Titled "Wrap It Up," it was written by David Porter and Isaac Hayes, and recorded in the late 1960s by Stax recording artists Sam and Dave, who had scored big with "Soul Man."

Kim wrote or cowrote seven of the ten songs that found their way onto the album. They played most of the songs every night on the road, but they sounded so retro that few people ever realized that Kim had written them. Before leaving Austin, they had to decide about using horns on the album. They decided against it, instead asking Roomful of Blues keyboardist Al Copley to join them at the studio. At the time, Copley was living in Zurich, Switzerland, with several members of Los Lobos.

Unlike the last album that Stevie had recorded live in the studio, the T-Birds wanted to use modern technology to build their album brick by brick. They started laying down the rhythm track, using just Fran's drums, Preston's bass, and Jimmie's rhythm guitar part, sometimes adding Copley on keyboards. The idea was to build a solid foundation, then allow Kim to add his vocals and Jimmie his guitar solos and flourishes.

Kim didn't tell anyone about "Wrap It Up" until they got there. He was hooked on the song the moment he heard it in the sampler. "Every song that comes out these days, hit songs, uses the Stax format," he explained. "That must have been in the back of my mind. I was going through about one hundred songs and it just stuck in my mind. I thought it was one of the best songs I had ever heard. . . . I just kind of sprung it on the guys. We rehearsed it once, and, boom, it had a fresh feel. Sometimes that works and sometimes it doesn't. With a cover version, I think the best thing is to listen to it once and then let it go. I don't feel like anyone can ever do it as well as the original artists."

That song was easy for them to record since they had the original Stax arrangement to go by. Not so easy was the song that Kim had written on the flight over, "Tuff Enuff." "Kim had some basic lyrics . . . [but] we went in there and the whole band transformed it into a song," recalled Preston. "When Kim brought it in, there was no bridge. We changed some of the lyrics. Kim was the frontman, but it was pretty much equal. No one ever tried to dominate musically. If you look at leadership, it was Jimmie and Kim. They started the band and they were the driving forces behind it. It was one of those chemistry things."

Fran remembers it pretty much the same way, though he credits Edmunds with putting the "garnish" on it. "He could draw things out of the band we had never really thought of before, point us in the right direction," he said. "He made it a challenge."

Once it was finished, "Tuff Enuff" was unlike anything else they had ever recorded—a gritty groove tune that was dressed up with unexpected chord changes and a drum part that was pulled up close to the listener's face. It has a hypnotic guitar part that Jimmie provided with a six-string bass and overdubbed guitar parts, and an unrelenting vocal that Kim poured his heart into.

The only cover songs they included were "Wrap It Up," Rockin' Sidney Zydeco song, "Tell Me," and "Why Get Up," a song composed by Bill Carter and Ruth Ellsworth. All of the other songs were T-Bird originals. The best of those were "Down at Antone's," an instrumental credited to all four band members, and "Look at That, Look at That," another composition for which everyone received credit. For that song, which had a late 1950s rock feel to it, Edmunds brought in Rolling Stones keyboard player Chuck Leavell, who played piano as Kim wailed away on his harmonica. For his solo, Jimmie played it smooth and simple, adding not a note more than was needed.

Not until it was obvious that the studio experience was going to proceed well did the band members relax and start enjoying their surroundings. "We took one night off in the midst of recording, were picked up at our flats by two Mercedes limos, and were driven out into the English countryside to Eric Clapton's estate for his fortieth birthday party," Preston wrote in his unpublished autobiography, "Into the Abyss." "We were met at the door by Patti Boyd, Layla herself, ex-Mrs. George Harrison and current Mrs. Eric Clapton, looking beautiful and a bit matronly . . . Liveried waiters wandered around serving some kind of highbrow Champagne and hors-d'ouevres. No dope of any kind in sight, though I was hoping. No matter. It was a wonderful night, mixing it up with so many of my idols from my youth."

Less than two weeks into the session, the good times came to an abrupt halt when a $50,000 check sent to Edmunds by the record company bounced. All of a sudden, they plummeted from the top of the world, where Eric Clapton lived in magnificent luxury, to the basement, where their blues heroes from the Delta had spent most of their lives. They had an unfinished album and no label to release it, even if it had been finished. Deeply embarrassed, petrified by the long-term implications, and overwhelmingly depressed, as only musicians can be, they gathered together to find a solution.

"Now it was, what are we going to do?" said Fran. "The studio wouldn't give us the master until we paid them. We had to decide what we were going to do. We had two choices—can the record or go find the money."

The T-Birds decided on the latter. Recalls Fran: "What we had to do, after spending six weeks making the record and living on tuna fish sandwiches, we had to go out and pull a tour together through Europe and Scandinavia to raise money to get the record out of hock—and that tour was something else! We pretty much did it by the seat of our pants and went back and got the record out of hock."

When the T-Birds returned to the States, manager Mark Proct started shopping the album with the major labels. Every one of them turned it down. They were debating their next step when a Toronto movie production company contacted them and offered an inexpensive video deal. The movie company had never done a music video, but it wanted to add that genre to its repertoire.

Figuring that they were in too deep to turn back, they used some of the money they made touring Europe to pay for the video. It was practically unheard of in America for bands to pay for their own videos, but the T-Birds didn't care what anyone thought. They had what they considered their best album and they were determined to do whatever it took to find a label for it.

They didn't go directly to Toronto but worked their way north, performing in nightclubs and music halls along the way. When they reached Toronto, they were surprised at how organized the production was.

"They had already cast and rehearsed a slew of gorgeous dancers, ran us through the paces, and it was done in a couple of days," Preston later wrote. "One of Toronto's most famous strippers was cast for the plum role in the middle of the video. Then, for the finale, they brought in one of the two existing police Harleys that were used for the pope's visit for me to ride across the set at the end of the video."

Armed with a new video, Proct returned to the record executives who had turned him down. This time he had a complete package—a finished album *and* a video. Finally Tony Martell at CBS Records made them an offer. The T-Birds were shocked because CBS had passed over the album twice already.

"We ended up financing the whole project and giving it to CBS," explained Kim. "It all got worked out between our banker and CBS."

The entire band went to New York to ink the deal, convinced that they were finally headed for stardom. The album would not be released by Epic, the CBS subsidiary that had signed Stevie, but by CBS Records.

To give themselves more of an edge when the album was released, the T-Birds hired Stevie's well-regarded publicist, Charles Comer, to spearhead the publicity effort. All record companies have in-house publicists to promote their products, but savvy recording artists usually hire outside publicists to supervise their publicity campaigns. At that time, Comer was one of the best.

Before their album *Tuff Enuff* was released, the Fabulous Thunderbirds joined forces with Stevie and Double Trouble for a tour of Australia and New Zealand that began in April 1986. Their first stop was in Auckland, New Zealand, the city where actor Russell Crowe developed his guitar chops.

They received a very warm reception in Auckland, which surprised no one. Sometimes referred to as the largest city in New Zealand, it has a population of only 150,000. Despite its relatively small size, Auckland has a strong rock 'n' roll tradition that produced a number of popular bands in the 1980s. Many people find that surprising, since for many years New Zealand limited the number of nonwhites who could enter the country.

Even today, there are very few people of African descent living in that country. In America, blacks are embraced by the music industry, and it would be difficult to imagine music without them; in New Zealand blacks do not even exist, except in the statistical census reports issued occasionally by the government.

The Fabulous Thunderbirds and Double Trouble arrived at their Auckland hotel by bus and were standing around at the front entrance, when a group of schoolgirls, all wearing eye-catching uniforms like the ones Catholic schoolgirls wear in the States, came walking by. Stevie's eyes honed in on one girl in particular—seventeen-year-old Janna Lapidus. She and her family had moved to New Zealand from Russia when she was a child. Strikingly beautiful, with dark, soulful eyes, she had begun a successful modeling career while still in high school.

"Stevie was love struck," recalled Preston, who is quick to point out that they were all drunk at the time. "He said, 'God, I love that girl!' Somehow he met her and they fell in love. She was a sweetheart. It was real love. It was amazing. Stevie was like, 'I'm going to marry that girl.' I was like, 'Ahhhhh, let's have another drink.'"

When they moved on to Australia, Stevie took Janna with him, although Preston insists that they slept in separate rooms. Stevie's marriage was in deep trouble at that point, but he still called home on a regular basis to talk to Lenny. He was no quitter. If anything, he tended to hold on too tightly to those he cared about. He never gave up on his father, despite years of abuse from him. Stevie never gave up on Jimmie either, not even when he was too busy or too indifferent to spend time with him.

To Stevie, Janna represented everything in life that was pure and true. He clung to her, intoxicated by her youthful beauty and her unspoiled innocence, qualities that were magnified all out of proportion by the cocaine and whiskey that he guzzled like water.

By the time they moved on to Australia, both bands were out of control. "We almost got thrown off of the only airline, which was very important to the tour because the country is so huge we couldn't get to our gigs without a jet," recalled Fran. "Every time we got on [the jet], it was like a big party. We were all hooting and hollering and laughing and drinking more than we should and turning up Patsy Cline to twelve and the other people on the planes were not amused sometimes."

For Fran, it was the best of times and the worst of times. "Being on the bill with our best friends—you're not just playing for yourself, you want to kick their butt, to give them a reason to give everything they have," he said. "Every gig was like a new event . . . and traveling between, you can image. All these crazy musicians were good friends and doing the tour together and we were all party animals.

"Actually, me and Wicker [a member of the tour] were the most sober and I'm not saying *we* were sober. We wanted to see some of the scenery, so we'd get out early and go see places or collect boomerangs, or go see the kangaroos." At that, he laughed. "We probably saw more of Australia and New Zealand than anyone else."

Toward the end of the tour, everything started falling apart. Stevie was so deeply into his cocaine and whiskey addiction that he was little more than a zombie. "One night his manager threatened to pull the plug," said Fran. "There were about four thousand people in the audience and Stevie had just gotten these new [amps] and he cut loose and I looked out at the audience. They were all sitting down, being polite. They didn't want to get up and be impolite. But I saw all the blood drain out of their faces and they turned white."

At times, Jimmie was just as unmanageable. It was painful for him to watch his younger brother implode before his very eyes. The only way he could cope was to get high himself. Stevie was at the height of his success. He had money and fame—and he was a basket case! What did that portend for Jimmie's future?

"[Jimmie] was going through upheaval times toward the end of that tour," recalled Fran. "I remember getting pretty angry at him at one point. He never missed a gig, but this one night, Doyle Bramhall was playing guitar with us and he had to play the whole night. I said, 'Hey, Jimmie, what are you doing? Either do it or don't.' He was just making decisions, trying to figure out what he wanted."

While they were on the tour, Stevie's manager, Chesley Millikin, told him that he couldn't take it any longer. He wanted out. Upon their return to the States, Stevie and Double Trouble asked Alex Hodges at International Creative Management in Los Angeles to be their manager and he agreed to do it, primarily because he liked Stevie and knew that he needed help with his career.

Hodges's credentials were impeccable. A former fraternity brother of Phil Walden, who gained fame as Otis Redding's manager, Hodges served as Redding's booking agent until the singer's death in 1967. Devastated by Redding's death, Hodges quit the music business and went to work for the Republican Party, where he stayed until late 1969, when Walden sent him a tape of a new band he was managing named the Allman Brothers. Intrigued by their gritty southern rock, Hodges left the GOP and rejoined Walden, who by that time had started a record label named Capricorn. Soon Hodges was managing a booking agency that represented the Allman Brothers, the Marshall Tucker Band, the Charlie Daniels Band, and Hank Williams Jr. In time, the agency also took on Stevie Ray Vaughan and Double Trouble.

Eventually Hodges shut down the booking agency and moved to International Creative Management, where he continued to serve as Stevie's booking agent. When Stevie told him that Milliken had resigned, Hodges compiled a list of recommended agents for Stevie's consideration, only to be told that it was Hodges that he and the band wanted. Hodges transferred the band's booking responsibilities to another agent at ICM and resigned to become Stevie's full-time personal manager.

After their return from Australia, Stevie hung out in Los Angeles for a while, afraid to go home to face Lenny. While he was in L.A. decompressing, Epic informed him that it was time to do another album. That was the last thing in the world that Stevie wanted to do. It seemed like only yesterday that they had recorded *Soul to Soul*.

But what could he do? He didn't feel like doing another album, but he didn't want to damage the great relationship he had with Epic.

After batting the idea back and forth a few times, he and the band decided to record a live album, one that could be done in a day or so.

For the Fabulous Thunderbirds, the return to Los Angeles was meant to be an opportunity for the guys to do something nice for their wives, whom they hadn't seen in months. "We all flew our wives into L.A., because we had two days there," said Fran. "We were going to do some things and then fly to Chicago. We got in at six in the morning and all the wives were there, but we had to leave an hour later to do a photo shoot and then it was on to Chicago. We only got to see the wives for about an hour. [By then] they had pretty much lost the excitement."

When Stevie returned to Austin, his greeting was not what he had expected. "The house was padlocked, the electricity had been shut off, the dog was missing, and Lenny was nowhere to be found," according to authors Joe Nick Patoski and Bill Crawford. "She's squandered his road earnings on dope while running around with other men that one acquaintance glibly described as 'police characters.'"

Stevie's life had become a nightmare, in every sense of the word. With his marriage in a shambles, he had no one to turn to for support, except for his band. Tommy Shannon became his constant companion. Whenever Stevie took a step, Tommy took a step. They were inseparable. That was good in the sense that it gave both men a sense of refuge, but it was bad in that it made it impossible for either man to curtail his alcohol and drug intake. One enabled the other.

In mid-July 1986, Stevie and Double Trouble performed for two consecutive nights at the Austin Opera House for the purpose of recording their live album. Rather than spend weeks in a recording studio, they thought they would simply play two performances, cull the best numbers for the album, and be done with it.

Unfortunately it didn't work out that way. For starters, the performances were tainted by Stevie's drug use, which escalated because of his problems with Lenny. His handlers went though the concerts fearing that he would fall over or pass out at any moment. He still played with fiery intensity, but he often made mistakes and he sometimes played so fast that his music was like an electric mixer, purring nonsense and white noise, all at thunderous sound levels.

From Austin they went to Dallas, where Stevie and the band performed at Starfest, before yet another enthusiastic crowd, with the recording equipment running the entire time. It was no better there, just more of the same. Because the tapes they ended up with were largely unusable because of technical or musical mistakes, they started booking studio time so that they could clean up the mistakes by overdubbing new parts.

The overdubs proved to be most difficult. Every time they fixed one part of the tape, another glaring error popped up. They ended up rerecording the entire album, piece by piece, surely the worst way possible to put together an album.

Stevie tried to carry on with his life, but the unfinished album kept intruding, pushing other projects to the side. Once envisioned as a quick way to satisfy his record contract, it slowly morphed into an albatross that threatened to ruin his life.

"Stevie told me, 'I don't even remember being in the studio making that record,'" says producer Jim Gaines. "He said, 'We were so screwed up. One day I woke up in a van outside the studio with all the doors open and I don't remember how I got there.'"

Gaines thought, "Wow! How could you make the whole record and not remember being there? That just shows you under what kind of conditions a lot of those records were made, being around a bunch of drug-induced people. They think the precision is there, but it's not."

During the Dallas concert, Stevie looked up to see Lenny standing backstage. She shouted at him, but he ignored her. She shouted some more and then started to walk onstage while he was playing. Two security guards rushed out and grabbed her and carried her away. As she left, she asked them to tell Stevie that she had come to deliver a message from his manager. Isaac Tigrett, founder of the Hard Rock Cafe chain, was giving a party in Stevie's honor at the Stoneleigh Hotel, she explained, and he wanted to present Stevie with one of Jimi Hendrix's guitars!

After the show, Stevie got the message. He met with family members, including his mother, who told him that his father's condition was getting worse. He visited with everyone, then left for the party at the Stoneleigh. He didn't like parties, but if someone wanted to give him one of Hendrix's guitars, that was fine with him.

Despite his association with Hard Rock Cafes, Isaac Tigrett was not well-known to the general public. His father, John Tigrett, was a prominent financial consultant in Memphis, and Isaac developed an interest in music while growing up in what local residents refer to as the "Bluff City," a reference to the fact that the city was built on a high bluff overlooking the Mississippi River.

Stevie went to the party with his cousin Connie, but he felt uncomfortable from the moment he entered the room. The room was filled with Dallas high-society types, people who made him uneasy, including actor Dan Aykroyd, who was there with his wife. Tigrett and Aykroyd were in the process of developing plans for a string of nightclubs called the House of Blues.

When Hendrix's Flying V guitar was brought out, Stevie handled it as if it were made of fragile glass and then began strumming and picking its strings, oblivious to the crowd gathered around him. Someone asked him to sign the guitar and he did, though without wondering why someone would ask him to sign a guitar that now belonged to him. After putting in a decent showing, he got up to leave and was headed out the door with the guitar when he was stopped by Tigrett, who asked him where he was going. It quickly became apparent that Tigrett had invited him there to show him the guitar, not give it to him. Outraged, Stevie let out a loud, "Fuck you!" and then stormed out of the room in a sullen rage.

Back in the limo, Stevie sat across from Connie, who took his hand and held it in an effort to calm him. "I said, 'Stevie, there are people like that in this world; don't let them get to you,'" Connie told Keri Leigh. "And he was totally sober by this time. He just sat back and said, 'You're right, Connie. You're always right, Connie,' and kinda rolled his eyes a little. We just laughed and blew it off."

Stevie thought that Tigrett had shafted him, but that was unlikely. Tigrett was well educated and had a privileged upbringing, and lying about a guitar to get a recording artist to his party was not his style. More likely, the message got garbled along its way to Stevie, not an unusual occurrence at that stage in his career.

Kim Wilson came to the door, his eyes slightly bleary from spending an hour alone with the Three Stooges. Cartoons flickered noiselessly across the television screen in his hotel room. It was midafternoon.

"I'm a little hoarse," he said. "A little conversation is just what I need to limber up my voice."

With his thinning hair, pencil-thin mustache, and stocky John Belushi body, Kim looked to the reporter who had come to interview him more like a Texas entrepreneur than a rock singer. But Kim was the real thing: a rhythm and blues holdout who has unapologetically refused to turn his back on his musical roots. The other T-Birds felt the same way. It's the main reason why, in the summer of 1986, they were the hottest R&B band in the country. Their album *Tuff Enuff* was headed for the Top 10, and two singles, "Tuff Enuff" and "Wrap It Up," had dragged the eighteen-year-old band's music into the mainstream.

Just don't call it roots or ethnic music in Kim's presence, because he says there's no such thing. "Roots music is a weird phrase to me," he explained, as music from a television cartoon created a soundtrack for the conversation. "I don't like it. Real music, I think, is a better phrase. People say that the popularity of our music is a sign of a R&B revival. I don't think that is true. I think people just want something that is honest."

Rhythm and blues is the best music there has ever been, he said—and to hear him tell it, it's not going to stop being played, not ever. "Our success could go away tomorrow, but I would still be playing this music. People in the eighties are finally getting a little more hip to what's bullshit and what's not. I think there's room for everyone. The problem with a lot of today's music is that everyone is trying to be so original, they're not playing anything. Everyone is trying to use stupid, little weird voices. It sounds like screaming alley cats to me. There are no human voices in rock 'n' roll anymore. The only place you can find human voices is on the soul charts."

Kim's voice cracked. He turned his head to cough and caught a glimpse of the television cartoon. It held his attention for a moment, and then he resumed the conversation.

If there is a key to the success of the Fabulous Thunderbirds, he said, it is persistence. No matter how hard the times got in past years—and in Texas the times can get plenty hard on the nightclub circuit—the band continued to play the type of music they liked. Nothing fancy, no flashing lights or clouds of smoke. Just basic R&B.

"There's no better place to hone your craft than in the joints," he said. "Until a year ago it definitely was not peaches and cream for us all the time. At one point I just said to hell with it, I'm not going to have a straight job. It's my life and I'm going to play music."

That's why it didn't upset Kim to hear people refer to the group as an overnight success. Whatever people want to think is fine with him, as long as the success continues. "When you expand your audience, those people aren't going to know what you did before and they're going to think you're brand new," he said. "The label, the product, the audience—it's really a great feeling. It makes me feel like a kid in a candy shop."

Kim had nothing but good things to say about the way Epic handled their album release. "They stuck their necks out for us," he said. "Luckily, we have a good relationship with our label. At least so far. We would do anything for them."

As Kim was speaking, "Tuff Enuff," the single, was firmly in the Top 20, pushing aside records such as Bob Seger's "Like a Rock," Patti LaBelle and Michael McDonald's "On My Own," and Billy Joel's "Modern Woman." Industry insiders considered it a miracle of sorts, for the album itself was made up mostly of retro sounds that belonged in a distant decade. None of the smart money would have been wagered on the album.

The only downside to the record's success was the lawsuit that it spawned from former T-Bird bassist Keith Ferguson, who claimed that the band owed him money. He refused to settle out of court and ended up losing his case. Things were never the same again between Ferguson and the band. Lawsuits have a way of poisoning the water.

Although it had been a year since the T-Birds recorded *Tuff Enuff*, Kim said he hadn't reached the point where he was tired of hearing the songs. "I can still listen to the album and that's a big thing for me. Usually I don't want to hear it so many times . . . but I never get tired of this one. Naturally, your first hit is kinda' dear to you."

Kim paused, savoring the moment, then he broke into a smile. "I guess you can call it a hit, can't you?" Again, he paused, this time longer than before, allowing the cartoon music to fill the void. "I just love to hear that word," he said. "Hit—."

Later that day, the Fabulous Thunderbirds performed at the Memphis fairgrounds, where the city's annual MusicFest was held. It was hot and sticky while the T-Birds were on stage, the temperature hovering in the mid-nineties, but no one seemed to mind. The T-Birds played "Tuff Enuff" and broke into smiles when the crowd roared their approval. Later they played "Wrap It Up," a special moment for them because they were in the city that had created that song and so many others.

Whether you called their music rock 'n' roll or soul didn't matter. They were in the belly of the beast that had invented both, performing at a venue that was one of Elvis's favorite places on earth. Really, did it get any better than that for a musician?

The Fabulous Thunderbirds didn't realize it at the time, but they were in Memphis during the most critical summer in the city's music history since the early 1970s, when everything fell apart. The city was swarming with musicians, magazine and newspaper writers, record label executives, and songwriters, all looking for the Next Big Thing.

The previous year, record producer Chips Moman had returned to the city to breathe new life into its long-dormant music industry. Mayor Dick Hackett arranged for him to use an abandoned fire station located near Beale Street, at the corner of Third and Linden, as the site for a recording studio. In addition, he was given a loan of $750,000 from the city to build a state-of-the art studio.

Hackett said he hoped the deal he made with Moman was going to be just the first of many. "The city has a lot of land scattered around," he explained. "There is some land on and around Beale Street, and if I can make a contribution on behalf of this community to entice recording studio[s] to come to Memphis . . . I will make a substantial contribution by coming up with the land or the buildings we have available. But it will have to be someone with a track record—someone who can produce."

Also caught up in the spirit of the moment were producer Willie Mitchell and Al Green, who had not recorded an album together since 1976. Inspired by the media attention the Memphis music industry was receiving, Green, who still lived in Memphis, called Mitchell and asked him if he would be interested in doing another album.

Mitchell jumped at the opportunity. Soon they were at work in the same studio that had turned out all of Green's hits in the 1970s. Green explained it this way: "What we want to see is if the quality is really there, and I mean from within. I want to see if I've really got it at this point in my life. They've told me I still do, but I want to see for myself." The resulting album, *He Is the Light*, was released in October 1985 by A&M Records. It didn't catapult Green to the top of the charts again, but it did set the mood for events that followed, especially Moman's high-stakes gamble to determine if Memphis "still had it" as a recording center.

Prior to starting construction on his studio, Moman put together a recording session that he felt would attract the sort of attention that he would need to rebuild the city's music industry. For an album to be titled *Class of '55*, he brought in the surviving members of the Sun Records glory years—Johnny Cash, Jerry Lee Lewis, Carl Perkins, and Roy Orbison—and, using mobile equipment, he arranged to record the session at the former Memphis Recording Service studio and at his old American Recording Studio.

"This album is an extremely important part of history," said Moman. "Sun Studio is a monument to music. It's not just history. It's a monument. It's important to me personally because I looked up to these guys for years. Our lives ran parallel, but we never got involved. Then down at the crossroads, we met."

The day before the session began, Moman held a press conference in the Peabody Hotel that was broadcast live by CNN and attended by the national news media, including *Rolling Stone* magazine.

Moments before stepping into the bright lights put in place by the television networks, Carl Perkins, probably best known for his hit "Blue Suede Shoes," confided to a reporter that he considered the session "one of those dreams that won't come true. I drove in by myself, and when I went past the studio on Union Avenue, it brought back memories. I haven't been in that studio since 1958. It's an emotional high I'm feeling. I just hope the album musically can live up to what I know the other three are capable of. I'm just going to be playing my old Fender the best I can."

The press conference was a historic moment in Memphis music. Just seeing Cash, Lewis, Orbison, Perkins, Sam Phillips, and Moman seated at the same table talking about music was a sight that veteran music writers never thought they would witness. That sense of awe spread to the participants themselves. Asked if the old Sun Records sound could be re-created, Cash said. "I think that sound could be duplicated if we have Sam Phillips close by to help us." At that, the room erupted into applause, causing Phillips to smile broadly. "We're here to recapture the spirit we had back then," Cash continued. "I think we all felt that spirit when we hit the city limits."

The session was as emotional as the press conference, as the four men relived experiences of thirty years ago. Each man recorded separately, using songs that each brought to the session, but on the final day they gathered together at American Recording Studio for a jam session on John Fogerty's song, "Big Train (from Memphis)." Joining the four artists were John Fogerty, who flew into Memphis to attend the session, Rick Nelson, Sam Phillips, June Carter Cash, Dave Edmunds, Ace Cannon, and the Judds, Naomi and Wynonna.

The album was recorded in less than a week under very difficult working conditions. No one was more surprised at the session's success than Moman. "I am still in awe of the fact that it happened," he explained. "Looking at it now, it's hard for me to visualize that it could be done. If I had this to do all over again, and know what I know now, I would see reasons to say, 'This could never be accomplished.' Because I didn't know it couldn't be accomplished, I guess, is why it happened."

The *Class of '55* recording session ended on an exuberant note, but that high point quickly evaporated after the album was mixed and submitted to major record labels. All of them ended up passing, not because they didn't like it but because the cost of acquiring the album—$1 million—was more than they wanted to pay. Johnny Cash's career was still going strong in Nashville, but none of the other participants had had a hit record in a long while. None of the major labels wanted to take a chance.

By February 1986, five months after the session concluded, it was obvious that the album was in trouble. PolyGram Nashville offered to distribute the album if Moman could put together a record label that could pay the million-dollar-plus production costs. Because interest in the album was so high in Memphis, Moman was able to find enough investors to establish a record label, which they named America Records. Its first product would be *Class of '55*.

The company was composed of an unlikely assortment of Memphis businessmen: Fred Smith, the founder of Federal Express, John Tigrett, whose son Isaac founded the Hard Rock Cafe chain, and three members of the Philip Belz family, which owned the Peabody Hotel and considerable real estate in and around Memphis.

The youngest Belz family member, Gary Belz, left his position at the hotel to play a prominent role in the company. "One of the things we see in the label is the possibility of making Memphis a major music center," he told a reporter. "We see more labels, more studios, more live music in Memphis as a result of America Records."

The Fabulous Thunderbirds's performance at MusicFest coincided with the release of *Class of '55*. The city was obsessed with the album, a fact that did not escape the attention of band members, who were frequently asked questions about Memphis music while they were in town, a result of their cover version of "Wrap It Up."

Kim took advantage of the publicity by announcing that he had started writing songs for a new album and was interested in hearing from other songwriters. "Mr. Porter," he said, a reference to David Porter, cowriter of "Wrap It Up" and countless other Stax hits, "If you're listening, I've always got my ears open."

The Fabulous Thunderbirds weren't the only musicians in town scoping out the city's music scene. Rolling Stones guitarist Ron Wood was on Beale Street to make a cameo appearance in a video for "Class of '55," the first single released from the America Records album. He told a reporter that he had been invited to the video shoot by Jerry Lee Lewis, who was scheduled to appear in the video with Perkins. "Hopefully, I will meet Roy (Orbison) and Johnny (Cash), too," he said. "I'm a fan of all of them."

During most of the video shoot, Perkins and Lewis often looked as if they felt sixteen again. That was especially true when Ron Wood showed up on the set. Some of the best moments of the shoot occurred inside a bus, away from the heat and the stares of passersby. Though the bus was crowded with bedraggled, sweat-soaked bodies, the continuous laughter helped everyone forget the miserable heat.

Wood almost couldn't believe he was on Beale Street. "Ever since I was a little boy, I remember W. C. Handy's name being thrown around by my older brothers," he said. "They were into jazz. They weaned me on Louis Armstrong, Big Spider Benton, Robert Johnson, and people like that."

For much of the shoot, Perkins was almost speechless. "Thirty-one years ago I wrote 'Blue Suede Shoes' in a little project house," he said. "I was so excited when I wrote it down. Even more so now when I hear it on the radio. But this is another world, to take a song and do something with it like we are seeing today . . . [I] wasn't ready for it to happen back then. I drank too much. I just wasn't ready. I don't know where all this is going, but I'm ready to ride it to see what happens."

Also caught up in the Memphis fever was Gregg Geller, the Epic Records executive who had signed Stevie Ray Vaughan to his first—and only—record contract. Not long after signing Stevie, he left Epic to take a position with RCA Records, where he was put in charge of that label's celebration of Elvis Presley's fiftieth anniversary, the most visible product of which was a series of new albums that contained previously unreleased material from the King's golden years.

"We here at RCA certainly are proud to have made that deal [with Sun Records for Elvis's contract], and it seemed to have been a good deal for everyone at that moment," said Geller. "But, my God, what might have happened had Presley stayed at Sun and managed to make the same breakthrough? We will never know the answer, but had it happened the history of Memphis music could have been very, very different."

In the summer of 1986, everyone associated with Memphis music was in a reflective mood, thinking nostalgically about what could have been and wondering what might yet be in store for the city.

Bob Taylor, president of the Memphis Federation of Musicians, was as optimistic as anyone. "When Chips Moman starts cutting at his studio there will be records on the charts, then people outside the city will look at that and start saying, 'Something is happening in Memphis.' And all the studios will get work."

In August 1986, Stevie and Double Trouble returned to Memphis to participate in a television pilot for the local PBS affiliate. Named

American Caravan, the program was meant to be a Memphis version of *Austin City Limits.* Guitarist Lonnie Mack, whose instrumental version of "Memphis" was a Top 10 hit in 1963, was asked to host the program, which was scheduled to be shot at the Orpheum Theater.

Stevie and Double Trouble were supposed to be the featured guests, but before taping began, Stevie received a telephone call from his mother, informing him that Big Jim was in a Dallas hospital, where he was losing his battle with Parkinson's disease. Stevie rushed to the airport, leaving Tommy Shannon and Chris Layton behind in Memphis to explain his absence.

Brown Burnett, a writer for *Nine-O-One Network,* a new music magazine based in Memphis, went to the Peabody Hotel to interview Stevie but discovered that he was gone. Instead, he spoke briefly to Shannon and Layton, who told him that they felt they had been working too hard lately. They confided that they were concerned about Stevie.

Memphis Caravan was taped as planned, but without Stevie or Double Trouble. Mack, then forty-five, told the story of how "Memphis" became a hit for him. "It was really an accident," he explained. "Dumpy Rice was playing piano in our band and he used to sing that song. Well, something happened where Dumpy wasn't there one night and we were getting so many requests for the song, we had to play it. Well, Dumpy was the only one who could sing it and since I didn't know the words, I played it as an instrumental and it evolved from there."

At the time, they were recording a song titled "Down in the Dumps." Needing a B side for the record, they recorded "Memphis," never expecting the song to be noticed. To Mack's surprise, a deejay in San Francisco liked "Memphis" better than the song he thought would be the hit—and it took off from there.

Mack's most recent album, *Strikes Like Lightning,* was produced by Stevie for Alligator Records in 1985. It was a contentious project because Stevie did not get along well with label president Bruce Iglauer, who found Stevie to be distant and "changeable" during the session, a likely result of the guitarist's heavy drinking and cocaine use. Iglauer later told interviewers that he wasn't used to seeing musicians being so flagrant in their drug and alcohol use.

Whatever the problems associated with making the album (Mack and Stevie and Iglauer all ended up unhappy with the project, but for different reasons) it did not affect Mack's friendship with Stevie. "Stevie has been great to me and he and I go way back," Mack told *Nine-O-One*. "When I was in Austin years ago, I was going from club to club looking for a guitarist who could sing tenor. Everyone told me to go see Stevie play. Well, I went in and heard him play and, sure enough, he was playing a lot of my songs. . . . Years later I ran into him again in a club in Louisville. He found out I was moving to Austin and that's when we decided to do an album together."

American Caravan failed to garner any interest for syndication. Mack did his best to be a good host, but without a star of Stevie's magnitude, the program was doomed at its inception. Mack and Stevie were good friends and shared a mutual respect, but, for reasons beyond anyone's control, their professional associations seemed to always end badly.

When Stevie arrived at the Dallas hospital, he joined Jimmie at Big Jim's bedside. Their father was only a shell of his former self. He had lost a great deal of weight and appeared very frail, quite a contrast to the robust, larger-than-life figure who had seemed so powerful in their eyes as children. By then, he had developed lung problems, the result of all those years spent working with asbestos; the coughing associated with the lung disease had caused him to have a series of heart attacks, which put him in the hospital.

Stevie and Jimmie sat with their mother at Big Jim's bedside, though he was unconscious and was being sustained by life support systems. Assured by doctors that the situation was hopeless, Martha gave her approval for doctors to turn off the machines. The day after the funeral, Stevie, badly shaken by his father's death, boarded a plane for a concert in Montreal.

Big Jim had been a major factor in both Stevie's and Jimmie's life, not always in a positive way. He encouraged their initial involvement in music but opposed it when he felt it was having a negative effect on their lives, leaving Martha caught in the middle between her husband and her sons. Later, when both brothers began to find success, their proud father embraced them again.

T-Bird bassist Preston Hubbard said that Jimmie and Stevie never talked much about their father when they were on the road. Occasionally they told funny stories about him, especially about his freewheeling domino games, which both brothers found hilarious. Big Jim attended some of his sons' performances in the early days, "but their mom came all the time," Preston said.

After the concert in Montreal, Stevie and Double Trouble went to Europe, where they began a tour that would end in disaster for Stevie. He had been in bad shape ever since his father's funeral. Shortly after they arrived in Germany, Stevie started coughing up blood. Chris Layton urged him to get medical treatment, but Stevie assured him that what he really needed was a drink of whisky.

Frightened by that turn of events, Chris called their manager, Alex Hodges, in a panic and told him that he needed to do something—and fast. Hodges acted quickly, abruptly canceling the band's tour responsibilities and putting Stevie in the care of Dr. Victor Bloom, a London doctor who treated recording artists with addiction-related health problems.

Dr. Bloom told Stevie that the massive amounts of alcohol and cocaine he had consumed had eaten a hole in his stomach. If he continued to drink, he explained, he would die. He recommended a month-long stay at a London clinic for treatment for his medical problems, then further treatment at a rehabilitation center when he returned to the States. A very frightened Stevie Ray Vaughan did as his doctor suggested.

"As soon as I got into the hospital, I called my mother up and said, 'I don't know if you knew this was coming or not, but I am in the hospital and this is what happened,'" Stevie later explained to Ken Micallef. "'Where are you?' she said. I told her and she was there the next day. I called my girlfriend [Janna], who was gonna try to meet up on my birthday [October 3]. She hadn't seen me in six months because I had been on a tear, didn't know how to act or what to be. She was there in two days."

After he completed his treatment at the clinic, Stevie agreed to do one last concert in London before returning to the States. It was a case of too much, too soon. Before the concert, he started drinking again. At the start of the performance, he told the audience that he was happy to be there: "You don't know how grateful."

Although he appeared pale and weak, everything went according to plan at the concert, with Stevie telling the audience that his mother was there with him. It was not until after the encore that trouble struck. Stevie was walking off stage wearing an Indian headdress, when he tripped and fell, receiving cuts and scrapes and several bad bruises.

Afterward he told interviewers that he didn't remember how many drinks he had that night because it was all a blur. If there was any doubt that Stevie was in a life-threatening situation, it was tossed aside when Stevie fell off the stage. The message was clear to everyone: If Stevie didn't get help soon, he would die.

Stevie stayed another five days in London, recuperating from his fall, and then prepared to fly to Atlanta, Georgia, where arrangements had been made for him to enter Charter Peachford, an addiction treatment center. Before they boarded the plane, Stevie borrowed $10 for cigarettes from his mother and went to a bar and spent it on booze.

"Here I had just come out of the clinic in London, had gotten some information about what was wrong with me, learned all about what the problem was and how to deal with it, and still fell right back into that old thinking," he later told *Guitar World*. "I mean, I was on my way to go into a treatment facility, yet my first thought was, 'Wow, I've never done this straight before [flying].' That's the type of thinking that we alcoholics have to defend against for the rest of our lives, though we take it one day at a time. Take care of today—that's the idea."

When they arrived at the treatment center, Tommy Shannon checked himself in as well. "Deep down inside, I knew that someday I was going to hit that brick wall," Tommy explained to the *Dallas Observer*. "Stevie and I hit it right about the same time. Chris and Reese were not as addictive in nature. They would drink with us, but they would wake up the next day and not do it. Take some aspirin and go on with their lives. We never stopped. We never had a hangover because we never stopped. There was no human power that could help us."

Stevie stayed in the treatment center about a month, not as long as doctors wanted him to stay but long enough to clear his head and convince himself that beating his addiction was a life-and-death matter for him. Part of the treatment involved participation in the twelve-step program developed by Alcoholics Anonymous.

After leaving treatment, Stevie continued working the twelve-step program, which called for him to attend daily AA meetings in whatever city he happened to find himself. Anonymity is the key part of the AA program. Members identify themselves only by a first name or pseudonym, not only protecting their individual identities but also "leveling the ego," as the literature says. There are no stars, celebrities, or "famous" people in AA. Every person is rendered equal with a common purpose: to get sober and to stay sober.

Stevie agreed to that condition, but later found it difficult not to discuss his addiction with interviewers. He soon became as obsessed with talking about his addiction as he had been feeding it with alcohol and cocaine, not an uncommon occurrence among addicts fighting for life. Stevie felt he had faced death and stared it down. The best way to keep himself from backsliding, he concluded, was to talk about it.

Another essential ingredient in alcohol and drug recovery is understanding how the alcoholic and addict finds comfort in drugs and alcohol, locating the "triggers." "I found out that if I stayed loaded all the time, my ego got patted on the back, and I didn't have to worry about things that I should've been thinking about," Stevie told *Guitar World*. "It was more comfortable to run from responsibilities. There were a lot of things I was running from, and one of them was me. I was a thirty-three-year-old with a six-year-old kid inside of me, scared and wondering where love is."

Not only did Stevie's breakdown cost him the remainder of the concerts lined up for that year, it meant that he was not able to return to Memphis in mid-November to attend the Blues Awards Show sponsored by the Blues Foundation, which he was scheduled to cohost with B. B. King. The day before the show, officials announced that Stevie Ray Vaughan would be a no-show due to injuries he suffered in a fall during a concert. That wasn't the reason, of course, but it sounded better than explaining that he was busy with his addiction treatment.

Performing that night in addition to Robert Cray were B. B. King, Albert King, Carl Perkins, Bobby Bland, and Rufus Thomas. It is a shame that Stevie was unable to attend, for it was the sort of crowd he reveled in.

Robert Cray was the big winner that evening, taking home six Handys, the most ever won by an artist since the event began seven years earlier. "When I was asked to attend the ceremonies, they warned me I was going to win one," Cray said. "I didn't know we would win as many as we did."

Cray was one of the big beneficiaries of Stevie's success as a recording artist, for it opened the door for other blues guitarists, black and white, to be contenders on the pop charts. By the time he attended the blues awards, his single, "Smoking Gun," was on heavy rotation on MTV and charting well on pop, jazz, and R&B charts.

Walking along Beale Street, Kim Wilson was stopped in his tracks by a portly blonde with red cheeks who leaped from her late-model car. "Yoo-hoo!" she shouted, waving her arms as though she were flagging down a taxi. "I just love your music!"

Kim smiled and returned her wave.

"And I just love the way you play guitar," she crooned.

Kim whirled on his heels and continued walking. "They mean well," he said under his breath.

The Fabulous Thunderbirds were in Memphis with producer Dave Edmunds to record their second album together. For two weeks, they had kept a high profile, doing interviews with the local media, visiting music stores, and seeing the sights of the city. One night they played two sold-out performances at their downtown hotel, the Radisson, which had gained a reputation as a rock 'n' roll inn.

Kim marveled at the depth of talent in the city. A local band, Reba and the Portables, opened for them at the Radisson and Kim said the lead singer, Rebecca Russell, was so good that he went upstairs to watch television after hearing her sing a couple of songs. "That lady's got a good set of pipes on her," he said. "That's one way I'm superstitious. If someone is really good, I try to stay away from them. That's just the way I am. There's a way it sounds in your head when you're playing and there's a way it sounds while you're listening and you really can't mix the two, not on the same night."

Only weeks earlier, they had performed in New Orleans during Mardi Gras for an MTV event. "The Mardi Gras thing with MTV was fun, but I had more fun at the Radisson," said Jimmie Vaughan. "Chuck [Lavelle] played piano with us and Steve Cropper came up and scared the hell out of me. But, you know, I had to play anyway."

"It wasn't like any other gig," said Dave Edmunds.

"It was a nice break from the recording," added Jimmie. "We were sitting [in the studio] and we thought, 'Yeah, let's go play a gig.'"

It was Jimmie's idea to record their next album in Memphis. "I had never recorded here, and we had done it in London, in Los Angeles, in New York, and in Austin and Dallas, so we just decided to do it here," he explained.

"We came because of the people, the players here," said Edmunds, who added that he had already made plans to return for another project.

"It's magic here," said Jimmie.

The main reason that Kim wanted to record in Memphis, he said, was because of the city's long history of producing hit records. "We just wanted to get the vibes on it," he said. "I think there might have been some business reasons, too, though that's not my job. I just wanted to come here and record because so many great things have come out of this town. All the stuff I grew up on came out of this town. We seem to be fitting right into the picture."

When the T-Birds came to Memphis, they ended up recording at Ardent Studios, a midtown operation that had been up and running since 1966. Founded by John Fry while he was in high school—he had two partners in that early venture, John King and Fred Smith, who went on to found Federal Express—the studio was first located in Fry's grandmother's sewing room.

Unlike many studio owners, Fry's ambition was not to make music himself (he had discovered early on that he didn't possess the necessary talent), but to build the best studio possible, with all the bells and whistles necessary to compete with the best studios in the South. By the early 1970s, he had facilities that surpassed those at Stax, American, and Hi. During the glory years of its existence, Stax often sent its overflow artists over to Ardent, where they had more up-to-date equipment.

The T-Birds were shocked to learn that another famous Texas band, ZZ Top, had recorded almost all its albums at Ardent. ZZ Top discovered the studio almost by accident. Together as a band since 1969, ZZ Top hit rock bottom by 1974, a year that they were booked at the Memphis Blues Show, a low-paying gig that offered neither fame nor fortune. While they were in town, they heard about Ardent and stopped by the studio, where they met staff engineer Terry Manning. One thing led to another and the band recorded its next album there and then continued to return year after year. During the late 1970s and 1980s, it was one of the best-kept secrets in the music business.

"I would like to be able to tell you that what we offer them is so unique they could not get it elsewhere," said John Fry. "We offer them good facilities and do a good job for them, but . . . frankly to be really honest with you those records could be made at the North Pole and still be popular. There is a factor of the chemistry of the people working together, but I cannot paint a picture that would say ZZ Top could not live without Memphis."

Fry displayed more humility that the law probably allows, but the truth is that ZZ Top's first albums recorded at Ardent did very well and the band continued recording at the studio because, whatever the source of the magic they found in Memphis, they didn't want to lose it, not while sales receipts were still pouring in.

The T-Birds hoped they would find the same magic at Ardent. One way to hedge their bet was to invite the Memphis Horns, the musicians who had played on all the Stax hits, and songwriter David Porter, who penned "Soul Man" and many other hits during the 1960s and 1970s.

Usually the Memphis Horns consist of only two players, Andrew Love on tenor sax and Wayne Jackson on trumpet, but for the T-Bird album they brought in two players who often worked with them, Jack Hale on trombone and Jim Horn on baritone sax.

Love, who was raised in Memphis, and Jackson, who was raised in West Memphis, have become metaphors for the Memphis experience. Love is black. Jackson is white. Although both men grew up in and around Memphis during the segregation era, they put that history aside whenever they went into the studio. The "sweet soul" that was so much a part of the Stax mystique was a by-product of their willingness to break new ground as a racially integrated team.

"We've always been proud of the fact that Andrew and I have never had any problem with the race thing," Jackson told Brown Burnett. "I can think of only one isolated incident when someone gave us a hard time. But it was so long ago and so insignificant."

Although the two men possessed all the ingredients for a definitive sound, it didn't come together fully until they started working with Otis Redding. "He was just one of those rare individuals who could walk into a studio and know exactly what he wanted," said Love. "Man, he could make a sound just like a horn and his ideas always worked. The things we learned from Otis shaped our sound and still do today. And he didn't even play a horn or read music that I knew about."

"With a horn player, you can't settle for anything less than the best and those guys [the Memphis Horns] just blew me away," said Kim. "It was entertaining to watch them work. I just sat here, drank beer, and watched them play. I told myself, 'You'd better keep your mouth shut; anything you can think of, they probably thought of years ago.'"

Edmunds seconded that observation. "I always thought the horns on the old Stax records sounded so unique and I wondered how they did it. Now I've worked with them and I still don't know."

Of the ten songs brought to the session, four utilized the Memphis Horns for maximum effect. "Stand Back," the lead cut on the album, featured them in a style reminiscent of the albums they recorded in the 1960s with Sam and Dave. Also added to the session was Rolling Stones keyboardist Chuck Leavell, who played organ and re-created the sound that Booker T. Jones had patented at Stax.

The Memphis Horns also played on Kim Wilson's "Wasted Tears," an Otis Redding–style ballad on which Love played a riveting sax solo, "Streets of Gold," another song penned by Kim, which featured Leavell on piano, and Kim's "Sofa Circuit," a song that was driven almost entirely by the interplay between the horns and the organ.

Of the ten songs used on the album, Kim wrote seven. One of them, "Hot Number," was used as the title for the album. Jimmie played a sizzling guitar lead on that song and tried to re-create the big-money feel of their biggest hit, "Tuff Enuff."

"Don't Bother Tryin' to Steal Her Love from Me," written by Roomful of Blues guitarist Duke Robillard, featured both Jimmie and Edmunds on guitar, along with Leavell on piano. Oddly, it was one of the few songs in the album on which Jimmie was allowed to really cut loose on his guitar.

"I wanted this album to be more diverse than the last one," explained Kim. "We've got some Stax-type stuff, some rockers, and we might have a little Jimmy Reed and a ballad or two. I don't like to talk about the songs too much. I'm like the baseball pitcher going out to the mound. I never step on the first base line." Thematically, he said, the album contained the usual T-Bird themes—"money and women, the surplus of and the lack of."

Talking about the album brought Kim to a point that really irks him. Not long after they arrived in town, the T-Birds discovered many local people were not familiar with the musicians that had made Stax famous the world over. He didn't understand why Memphis musicians are ignored in their hometown.

"That really gets me," Kim said. "Some of the people I've met here have made some of the best records ever made. People get taken for granted. I know that happens in a lot of towns, and I can take it happening to me, but when it happens to people of the stature I've met here, I can't handle that.

"They should be put on a pedestal in this town. As nice as this town is, I really believe there are a lot of people here who don't even know who these guys are. I don't know whose fault that is, but I know it ought to change."

At one point, Kim, Jimmie, and Edmunds broke away from work at the studio—Fran Christina and Preston Hubbard had left town after putting down a rhythm track—to receive a belated award at a local restaurant. The Fabulous Thunderbirds had received a Handy at the previous ceremony, the one that Stevie Ray Vaughan was not able to attend, but they had not yet received the trophy.

Along with their manager, Mark Proct, Kim, Jimmie, and Edmunds piled into a minivan and raced across town to a Beale Street restaurant, tossed about like cabbages in a box, the result of the heavy-footed driver's enthusiasm to get them there in record time.

Peering out a side window, Kim observed, "Man, the people in this town drive like crazy." Told that Memphis was the traffic-light accident capital of the country, he said, "Really!"—and then began to eye the stop-and-go signals with new interest.

At the restaurant, they ate barbecue in a private backroom, interrupted periodically by autograph seekers, then went back into the main room, where they received their Handy award from Blues Foundation founder Joe Savarin.

Shortly after that took place, a pretty lady in a low-cut white dress strolled up to Kim and said, "Sing for me." She didn't ask—she *told* him to sing for her, as if the sight of her in a virginal white party dress would be enough to make him burst into song. He didn't. He smiled broadly to everyone in the room, then dashed through the kitchen and out into the night air.

Later that night, back at the studio, Edmunds joked that the theme of the new album was ecology. His comment was a put-down of artists who maintained, usually amid the glare of television cameras, that there was more to their music than simply music.

Although Jimmie often seems the most intense T-Bird on stage, he is one of the most easygoing. Asked if he was a perfectionist in the studio, he laughed: "You know, it seems to work best when I don't care."

"That's right," said Edmunds. "If you care too much, you can get sidetracked and lose track of the original idea. There's a fine line between getting all the notes right and getting it to feel right. You have to sort of balance it and make sure you get both."

Edmunds said he loved working with the T-Birds. "We talk the same language, really, and I understand what they're doing, although I come from a completely different culture," he said. "Different country and all that. I grew up listening to the music that these guys love. I love Memphis music and Stax and Sun Records, and so do these guys."

Jimmie echoed that sentiment: "We were just diggin' it. That's pretty much the way Memphis is to me. Just like that." He thought a minute, then he added, almost as an afterthought, "I want to make a record here with my brother."

No sooner did the Fabulous Thunderbirds leave Memphis than Stevie Ray Vaughan rolled into town to play a concert at an amphitheater at Mud Island, a city-owned park and tourist attraction located in the Mississippi River. One of the first things he did was find the nearest meeting place for Alcoholics Anonymous. The organization's twelve-step program had become the foundation of his new life.

Since recovering from his life-threatening addiction the previous fall, he had reevaluated his life and started putting it in order. While he was in the Atlanta hospital, he asked Lenny to visit him so that they could talk about their marriage, but she declined to do so. He wanted to repair his marriage, or so he thought.

When Lenny didn't bother to visit him in the hospital, Stevie filed for divorce, citing "conflict of personality," a charge she could defend in view of their many years together. She countersued, charging him with adultery, a charge he could not defend, considering his current relationship with Australian teen Janna Lapidus.

If Stevie thought that divorce was a problem that his lawyer could solve by having him sign a few papers, he was badly mistaken. Neither side was willing to agree on a settlement early on, so the proceedings dragged on and on, sucking the life out of Stevie's creative efforts. He had no problem performing; all he had to do was step into the spotlight with his guitar and let his talent do the rest. But writing songs was another matter, and he found it impossible to focus on that for the entire time of the divorce proceedings.

Even after walking through the fire of alcoholism and drug addiction—and all the dark alleys and bottomless pits that that had taken him into—there remained a childlike innocence about Stevie. He truly didn't have a mean bone in his body (unless he was drunk or high, and out of his right mind). He was devastated by the negative energy that surrounded his divorce and he tried to inject civility into the proceedings whenever possible, for his own peace of mind, if for no other reason.

"At one meeting, Stevie and I were sitting with all the lawyers around a table," Lenny told authors Joe Nick Patoski and Bill Crawford, "and Stevie was going on and on about how great I was and everything. I looked at him and said, 'Stevie, this really isn't the time to be talking about that.'"

Despite Stevie's best efforts, they were unable to reach a settlement, which meant that it had to be decided by the courts. In the end, Stevie only had to pay Lenny a $50,000 lump-sum payment (his concern at that time was cash flow), but the court awarded her a one-fourth interest in the royalties from his first four albums, which ended up being a substantial sum of money. He had to pay lawyers' fees of well over $100,000.

All things considered—Stevie had come to terms with his addiction, dealt with divorce, and lost his father, all in the space of a year—the guitarist was in remarkable spirits when he arrived in Memphis. On the afternoon after his arrival, Brown Burnett, a local newspaperman, went to Stevie's downtown hotel to interview him for *Nine-O-One* magazine. With him was the magazine's publisher, who shot photographs of Stevie.

"I walked into his hotel room and he was standing there smiling really big," Burnett later recalled. "He grinned and said, 'I got new teeth.' He looked great—rested, fit, dressed up (no hat). He looked and talked like a completely new man compared to the worn-out, worn down guy I first met in 1984."

"Guitar hero. Every generation has one, sometimes even two or three," Burnett wrote in *Nine-O-One*. "Chuck Berry, Keith Richards, Pete Townshend, Les Paul, Leadbelly, Hendrix, Segovia—all are guitar heroes, role models to be emulated, imitated and analyzed. The label usually comes in the twilight of a career, at a time when the artist has more past than future, but there are exceptions. Consider Stevie Ray Vaughan. On a mellow, Memphis afternoon, with white sunlight ricocheting off the skyline, he is all spit and polish. In his prime. He's probably wealthy, certainly healthy, wearing his Guitar Hero label with a big grin. He is on the road again, this time in the middle of what he called a 'loopdeloop' tour, swinging him from the Northeast, out West and back again."

"I love to work," Stevie said. "And I love the work. Even when I take time off. Then I get back to work and think about what I didn't do."

Before coming to Memphis, Stevie started out the year by playing at the State Fair Coliseum in Dallas with Lonnie Mack and Omar and the Howlers—Omar being Kent Dykes, the Mississippi-born guitarist that Stevie once described as "the real thing, and I'm sure he'll always be the same. Success won't change him at all. You know, it's funny, but I bet Howlin' Wolf was a lot like Omar—larger than life."

The Dallas concert was the first time he had ever played sober in that city, and he was amazed at how good he felt. Instead of lecturing about the ills of the world, he talked to his audience about the wonderment of feeling good without alcohol or drugs. Good health, physical and mental, became a cause for him, something besides music that he could believe in and measure his life against.

In April, Stevie was a guest on the Cinemax special, *B. B. King and Friends,* along with Albert King, Etta James, Eric Clapton, Paul Butterfield, Phil Collins, and others. Sadly, Butterfield died a few days after the show was taped. He was only forty-four. "I saw that he wasn't real happy," Stevie said. "He and Albert King weren't hitting it off too well. The stage was set in the middle of the room and all the amps faced each other and we all played to each other and Paul's amp faced Albert's mic. Albert likes certain things. He doesn't like bass drums too loud, doesn't like harmonicas too loud. He wants his vocal mic loud and he doesn't want all the guitar players to play too loud.

"Don't get me wrong, there were no major things, but when you have that many musicians at once [things happen]. If there was a solo, there would sometimes be four guitars up there to play a twelve-bar solo. When everybody is trying to minimize frustrations and still play what they want to play, there are going to be a few remarks made here and there. No big deal. I could see that Paul was having a hard time, the same way anyone would do after drinking and drugging for too long."

Stevie said he was enjoying working again, especially playing before live audiences. He also expressed satisfaction with working on the soundtrack for a movie titled *Back to the Beach* and appearing in Ron Howard's movie *Gung Ho*. "It's something I've always wanted to do, work on soundtracks, but everybody's making a big deal for the film, *Back to the Beach*. All I did was sing and play guitar. I guess that proves that I'm good at being myself, huh?"

Stevie said he tried not to think about how the public perceived his work. "That's really not why I work so much," he explained. "It's more like I'm finally getting a chance to do things I've always wanted to do. . . . As far as keeping my head together and doing the things I really want to do, I'm finally seeing some light at the end of the tunnel."

During the interview with Burnett, Stevie put on his hat to pose for photographs in the window, talking the entire time. "I spend all of my spare time now working on myself and trying to keep from being so troubled inside," he said. "It's helping. I'm finding out that the worst days today are better than the best days used to be. I just want to straighten myself out. I've missed a lot, looking back on things. I even have a house now, even if I do rent it, and I hope to spend some time there eventually."

After the photographs, Stevie sat on the sofa to continue his conversation with Burnett. Now there was a stern look in his eye. He wasn't angry, but he was more intense than when the interview first began, as can be seen in a photograph of the two talking.

"Lately, what gives me the most good feelings and it may sound corny to some people, I've been working on this program that keeps me from drinking," he said, giving Burnett a look letting him know that he knew a fellow alcoholic when he saw one. "It's almost all of my spare time. I'm trying to learn about and work on it myself. No matter what I'm doing, I'm still trying to push some feeling back, you know, and it seems to be helping a lot. The worst day now is a hell of a lot better than the best days when I was hurting myself."

Burnett tried to change the conversation by asking another question, but Stevie would have none of that and came back to the topic that he obviously thought his interviewer should hear. "For me right now, it's just trying to learn more about straightening myself out," he said. "If I'm doing the best I can at doing the right thing, then all I'm really doing is putting forth that little bit of effort doing what should be done and the rest is taken care of. Therefore, I end up getting the most done by just keeping myself in the right spot."

After the interview was over, Stevie picked back up on the issue. He was relentless in a quiet sort of way. Recalled Burnett: "We had a great interview and had fun talking about music and mutual friends and acquaintances, but he kept coming back to his new-found sobriety and how much it had changed him and his life for the better. He called it a 'miracle.' He told me how he 'bottomed out' and made the decision to clean up, all in great detail and with much passion. He kept coming back to the sobriety thing. It sorta pissed me off a little. I became annoyed a bit, but what the heck, it was his interview."

A couple of hours after the interview was over, Stevie was driven over to Mud Island to do a sound check before that evening's performance. It was hot that day, very hot, but Stevie wore a dark suit and his famous hat, while the other band members were dressed in jeans and T-shirts.

After strumming his guitar a couple of times to hear the sound level, he looked out at the slow-moving river with awe. Behind him was the Memphis skyline, pretty much the same silhouette that greeted Elvis and Johnny Cash and Jerry Lee Lewis and Otis Redding and Albert King and Howlin' Wolf and too many others to count. He looked at a nearby photographer and grinned broadly, feeling the Memphis *thang* tremble beneath his feet.

By 1987, the new Memphis music revolution was in full stride. Although Chips Moman's *Class of '55* album didn't move up the charts as expected, it did attract other artists to the city. The first artist Moman recorded after *Class of '55* was soul singer Bobby Womack, with whom he had had several hits in the late 1960s, including "Fly Me to the Moon" and "California Dreaming."

Moman was understandably nervous about the session. "I'm nervous on the start of every session I do, but I was extraordinarily nervous with Bobby this time because I didn't know whether the studio was going to go up in smoke," he said, referring to the fact that it was the first session in his new studio, which he had named Three Alarm because it was housed in a former fire station. "But, you know, I couldn't think of anyone I would rather try to get a hit with than Bobby. He's got a distinct style. He's a great singer, writer and guitar player. That's about all you could ask for. He's also one of the best arrangers of horns I've ever heard in my life."

For Womack, the decision to return to Memphis after eighteen years was a tough one. First, because he didn't understand why Moman picked him to be the first to record in the new studio. Second, because he couldn't explain his affection for the city to his family and associates, most of whom questioned the wisdom of leaving Los Angeles to do an album in Memphis. But it was the lure of the city, that much celebrated Memphis *thang*, and his respect for Moman's talents that won out.

"I had all the people on my end saying, 'What do you want to go to Memphis for?'" Womack explained. "I told them my music is what Memphis is all about. It's very peaceful, it's loving and caring, and the people there, the musicians, are like that. It's a magical place."

At the hotel one day Womack ran into his friend Stevie Wonder, who was in town for a concert. Wonder asked him what he was doing in Memphis. "I said, 'Stevie, this is where it's happening,'" Womack said. "I called him the next night at the hotel, and they said Stevie had gone to a studio."

Womack broke out into laughter. It was the type of situational humor he appreciated. The fact that Stevie Wonder questioned his acumen for recording in Memphis and then, when he thought no one was watching, hurried over to the nearest studio to tap into whatever it was that his friend Bobby was siphoning off, was enough to give him an upper hand with his friend. Ah, the psychology of making music!

"I go to where the soul people are, not just the people in the studio, but the people who walk the streets," Womack explained. "This is where you get the raw soul. You can come here and go to work. You can get inside your soul. In L.A. you have to lock the door to get inside your soul, and even then you can get caught up in the electronic slickness of what everyone else is doing. . . . This is the capital. You can't cut no bigger than Elvis and Al Green."

Womack's album *Womagic* was released in November 1986. To Moman's disappointment, the album stalled on the charts, even though reviews were encouraging. By the end of the year, Moman's record label, America Records, looked to be in bad shape. *Womagic* had been released by MCA, not America Records, and stockholders were anxious to get another product on the market.

In February 1987, ex-Beatle Ringo Starr arrived in Memphis to record an album at Moman's Three Alarm studio. There was some confusion about whether the album was for America Records or was one of Moman's private projects, but the session went well, with Starr's actress-wife Barbara Bach attending each day and adding a touch of Hollywood glamour to the proceedings.

Throughout the session, Ringo was extraordinarily relaxed and playful, snuggling during the playbacks with Barbara, who sometimes sat on his lap. Starr's voice surprised everyone, perhaps because he had always been described as the Beatle who couldn't sing. Memphis musicians were elated. An actual Beatle was recording in the city!

All that changed when Starr and his wife left town for a few days. While they were gone, a columnist for the local newspaper wrote an unflattering story that depicted Starr as an "aging Beatle." When the ex-Beatle returned to Memphis, he was greeted by a firestorm of publicity, as Moman and his wife and several friends formed a picket line on the sidewalk in front of the newspaper to protest the story.

As soon as the album was finished, Ringo threw a party aboard the riverboat *Island Queen*. Everyone who was anyone in Memphis music was invited. It was Ringo's way of saying thank you to Memphis. Starr didn't eat any of the barbecue served at the party. "It's my stomach," he explained. "Most of the things I eat now have to be broiled. I can't eat spicy food." Later he sat in with the band and played the drums. "I can't believe it!" gushed one partygoer. "I'm really seeing him play!"

Starr seemed perfectly happy when he left town and returned to Los Angeles. Upon receiving the first cassette of the session, he rented a limo so that he and some friends could drive around town and listen to his Memphis album. Unfortunately there was a problem. Said Ringo: "Wouldn't you know I'd get the only [frigging] limo in town without a tape deck!"

Later, for reasons that he never explained, Ringo changed his mind about the album and told Moman that he didn't want it released. The two men ended up in federal court in Atlanta, with each making charges against the other. In the end, the court barred the release of the album and ordered Starr to pay Moman for the studio time. No one was happy with that Memphis adventure, least of all Moman, who had counted on the album to bring publicity to Memphis.

Not affected by negative publicity over Starr's session, other artists rushed to Memphis to tap into the music scene. In October 1987, U2 arrived in Memphis to record at the old Sun Records studio, even though Sam Phillips no longer owned it. What the band had in mind was recording a song with B. B. King, whom they had met the year before in Dublin during King's Ireland tour.

"They came backstage after the show, like artists sometimes do," said King, describing their meeting. "When they were getting ready to go, I said, 'Sometimes when you're writing a song, why don't you write one for me.' Bono [U2 lead singer] smiled. I didn't hear from him for over a year and then one day my manager called and said he had just heard from Bono. He said he'd written a song for me."

Later, King learned that Bono had written a song for them to sing together, "When Love Comes to Town." The song was recorded in Sun Studios, along with two additional numbers, "Love Rescue Me" and "Jesus Christ." All three songs ended up on U2's next album, *Rattle and Hum*.

Ringo Starr and U2 weren't the only musicians to come to town that year. R.E.M. recorded an album, *Green*, at John Fry's Ardent Studio, as did the Replacements and ZZ Top. Attracted to all the studio activity was former MTV head Bob Pittman. After leaving MTV, he started up his own record label titled QMI Music. The first two acts he signed for the label were Memphis artists Ella Brooks, a black rhythm and blues singer, and Jimmy Davis, a young roots rocker in the John Mellencamp tradition.

As 1987 ended, Memphis was considered *the* place to record. The Fabulous Thunderbirds had the Memphis fever and Stevie Ray Vaughan's temperature was rising with each passing day, with Memphis looking more and more like the Promised Land.

CHAPTER 5

All Roads Lead
to Memphis

*H*OT NUMBER proved to be a disappointment for the Fabulous Thunderbirds. The album failed to chart the way its predecessor had, and reviews were less than enthusiastic. The T-Birds were baffled. They had tried to recreate the sound that had brought them so much praise on *Tuff Enuff*, even going to the trouble of embellishing it with the magic of the Memphis Horns. Where did they go wrong?

The failure of *Hot Number* made them reevaluate their priorities. Were they nothing more than a Texas bar band? Had *Tuff Enuff* been a fluke? Jimmie and Kim had always fought with each other— as brothers who knew they had to make up afterward for the family's sake. When they fought now, the disagreements took on a different tone. There was a hint of desperation in the air.

The blues had taken them to the top of the charts with *Tuff Enuff*, but there seemed no place to go after that. Kim enjoyed the success of a hit record and wanted more of the same. Jimmie wanted success too, but he also wanted to grow as a guitarist, just as Stevie had done. The question the T-Birds had to answer was whether they could grow and chase commercial success at the same time.

Asked to contribute an original song to the soundtrack for the Tom Cruise movie *Cocktail*, they returned to Ardent Studio in Memphis to record "Powerful Stuff," a song that Kim wrote with Robert Field and Wally Wilson. With a guitar introduction and a driving drum beat, the song was freakishly derivative of "Tuff Enuff," but without the down-under fire. Nonetheless, it found itself in some pretty good company on the soundtrack: Robert Palmer singing his hit "Addicted to Love," Little Richard singing "Tutti Frutti," and Ry Cooder taking on Elvis Presley's "All Shook Up."

The film, which costarred Elisabeth Shue and Gina Gershon, did not do well with the critics and did nothing to enhance Cruise's box-office appeal. *Chicago Sun-Times* critic Roger Ebert did not have much good to say about the movie, calling it "empty and fabricated." He particularly disliked a scene in which Cruise and another bartender flip bottles at each other like circus jugglers.

"All of this is done to rock 'n' roll music, and it takes them about four minutes to make two drinks," Ebert wrote. "They get a roaring ovation from the customers in their crowded bar, which is a tip-off to the movie's glossy phoniness. This isn't bartending, it's a music video, and real drinkers wouldn't applaud, they'd shout: 'Shut up and pour!'"

Regardless of what the critics thought about the movie, having a song in a Tom Cruise movie was reason enough to release an album, so Epic Records gave the green light to the T-Birds to return to the studio. Because "Powerful Stuff" had been recorded at Ardent, they returned to Memphis in November 1988 to record the entire album.

"I always loved Memphis music and I grew up listening to all the Stax stuff and the music that came out of Sun," said Fran Christina. Booker T. and the MGs drummer Al Jackson was his all-time favorite. "We did an album with Santana and Booker T. one time *[Havana Moon]* and we're doing this Memphis kind of groove and Booker T. is over there playing and he's got his eyes closed and every once in a while he'd open his eyes and look at me. I'm thinking to myself, 'Oh, shit—I know I'm screwing up and he hates it.' We went to lunch after that and I said, Booker you've got to tell me, man, you looked bothered when we were playing that song. He said, 'Man, I had to look up because I thought I was playing with Al Jackson. I said, 'Booker, that is the best thing anyone has ever said to me. I can die now—and from your mouth!'"

When the T-Birds returned to Ardent to record what would become the *Powerful Stuff* album, they did so without Dave Edmunds, the Memphis Horns, and Chuck Leavell on keyboards. Instead, they went with Ardent staff producer Terry Manning, who had made a name for himself working on the ZZ Top albums and on 1970s *Led Zeppelin III*. Not only did Manning produce the new T-Bird album, he played keyboards when necessary and served as the engineer.

Asked by *Billboard* why he wanted to record at Ardent, Jimmie said, "It's just a classic studio. You can get any kind of sound you want, because the rooms were designed well. You have the best of the new and the best of the old, too."

Powerful Stuff was different from other albums they had recorded for several reasons, the most obvious being that Kim wrote only four songs for the album—"Knock Yourself Out," "Emergency," "Powerful Stuff," and "She's Hot"—and two of those were cowritten with other songwriters. Kim's songs were throwbacks to 1950s-style rockers with dead-ahead drum beats and guitar solos with lots of distortion.

Kim collaborated on "Knock Yourself Out" with David Porter, whom he had met when they recorded their previous Memphis album. Porter's relationship with Stax was legendary. As a youngster, he tried repeatedly to get into the studio, only to be turned away because of his age and lack of musical credentials. He countered that by getting a job at a grocery store across the street from the studio. Every day after work he went into the record store that was adjacent to the studio and talked to Stax cofounder Estelle Axton, who was impressed by his determination.

One day, he took Axton a song he had written and asked for her opinion. "The song had eight sheets of words," she later recalled. "I said, 'No way, David. You have to concentrate it, shorten it.' I would play him records that were hits. Today, he gives me credit for teaching him how to write songs. It makes me feel so happy I helped someone. He and Isaac Hays are the best writers around."

Once he got his foot in the door, Porter met Hays and began writing songs with him, with David doing the words and Isaac composing the music. One of their first songs, "Hold On, I'm Coming," gave Sam and Dave their first hit.

For Fran Christina, having Porter come in and out of the studio while they were recording offered some of the best moments of the session. "Memphis has always been a part of my repertoire," he said. "As a matter of fact, I wrote my first song with David Porter. Porter was very funny. He told the story about 'Hold On, I'm Coming.' He was in the bathroom and they were calling to him—'Come on!'— and he kept saying, 'Hold on, I'm coming.'" Fran laughed just thinking about it. "He had the trots."

Porter wasn't the only veteran musician dropping in on the sessions. Eagles guitarist Joe Walsh also was a frequent visitor, as was Rolling Stones guitarist Ron Wood and Sun Records alumnus Jerry Lee Lewis, with whom the T-Birds once performed at a New Hampshire casino.

"We loved Memphis," said Preston Hubbard. "And Ardent Studios was great. We were very comfortable there. We always had friends there. Of course, we were all into substances then. It was kind of like a rolling party. We would go into the studio from maybe two until midnight, then hit the Peabody Hotel bar or something."

Also in Memphis during that time was actor Dennis Quaid and actress Winona Ryder, who were in Memphis to film *Great Balls of Fire!* Quaid played the role of Jerry Lee Lewis and sixteen-year-old Winona Ryder played his child bride, Myra Gale Lewis. The real-life marriage created a worldwide scandal in 1958, since Myra was only thirteen—and was his cousin.

Before the marriage took place, Jerry Lee confided in Elvis about his plans. At first Elvis thought it was a joke. When he realized that Jerry Lee was serious, he said, "God bless you Jerry Lee. You just saved my career." And that was just about the way it went down. Jerry Lee's career never recovered from the bad publicity and Elvis's career soared, even when he moved a teenager named Priscilla into his house.

Jimmie Vaughan, in what was clearly a case of being in the right place at the right time, was recruited for a minor role in the film as Roland Janes, an engineer who worked with Sam Phillips at the old Sun Studio.

The Fabulous Thunderbirds took such a liking to Winona that they performed at her birthday party (she turned seventeen while in Memphis). "Jimmie went out and bought her this huge, humongous teddy bear," said Preston Hubbard. "The whole cast and crew from *Great Balls of Fire* was there." Later Preston and a crew member from the movie took Winona out to a movie to see Dennis Quaid's newly released film, *Everybody's All-American.*

Winona had only made five films at that point, including *Beetlejuice* and *Heathers*, and she wasn't sure in the beginning if she could do the role justice. To her displeasure, the media had depicted her as a Lolita type, a characterization she despised. By taking on the role of Myra Lewis, she pretty much surrendered to that image. Even so, she fell in love with the character, as only a sixteen-year-old could. "Myra Lewis was probably the furtherest you could get from the real me," she told *Rolling Stone.* "But the thing I associated with was her strength, her honesty, and her love for Jerry Lee Lewis."

Since the film was based on Myra's autobiography, it offered her view of the marriage. It was a view that Jerry Lee Lewis disagreed with. He denied that he was head-over-heels in love with his cousin and he challenged her view that he swept her away from high school in his red convertible. He married Myra, he insisted, because he had made love to her and felt he had to live up to his obligations.

Great Balls of Fire! started out to be Jerry Lee's biography but ended up, for artistic reasons, focusing only on the first three years of his career. In an effort to obtain Jerry Lee's cooperation, producers sent Jerry Lee a copy of the script, only to have it returned with the word "lies" written on it. After some give-and-take, he eventually relented and agreed to work as an adviser on the film, primarily because he feared that someone else, probably some damned actor, would end up singing his songs if he was not there to protect his legacy.

As it turned out, Jerry Lee and Dennis Quaid strongly disagreed over who should sing the songs in the soundtrack. Jerry Lee felt that no one could do the songs justice but himself, and Quaid felt that he should do it to preserve the realism of the film. The two men went around and around, with Jerry Lee telling him he couldn't sing like Jerry Lee Lewis and Quaid telling him that he couldn't act like Dennis Quaid.

To prove that he could handle the vocals, Quaid rented studio time at Sun Studio and asked the Fabulous Thunderbirds to drop by and sit in with him. Fran was amazed when he walked into the studio and listened to playbacks.

"I said, 'Man, that sound is incredible," he later recalled. "The engineer said, 'You know what, I haven't touched a damn thing. This room is magic.' And it really was. Playing in there, it was so weird. I don't know what it is, but that place is magic. I have been in some of the best studios in the world and I've never heard raw sounds like that. I don't think anyone can explain it. If an acoustician went in there, they probably could figure it out. I guess it was just the spirits of what went on in there."

The T-Birds recorded seven songs with Quaid playing piano and singing. "It was great," said Preston. "I think most were cover tunes, but there might have been a couple of originals that Dennis wrote."

Even with the T-Birds' help, Quaid lost the battle with Jerry Lee. "Killer" did the soundtrack and Quaid was reduced to lip-syncing his way through the film. There were no hard feelings, though. When the movie was released, Jerry Lee had nothing but praise for Quaid's performance *as an actor*.

Critics were interested in the film, but not necessarily kind in their observations. Wrote Rita Kempley for the *Washington Post*: "*Great Balls of Fire!*, like *La Bamba*, is thin on the meaning of the life in question, but big on 1950s Billboard nostalgia. It's lightweight archaeology, a bent American Bandstand biography. Something slipped away . . . the truth, the heart, the soul. All that's left is the hip."

Peter Travers, writing in *Rolling Stone*, noted that the movie "can shake your nerves, rattle your brain and at the very least make you feel like dancing," but he took issue with the "candy-coated" gloss that the director put on the story: "Any which way you look at it, *Great Balls of Fire!* stacks up as something small, shriveled and inexplicably tame, Goodness gracious indeed."

While the Fabulous Thunderbirds were recording *Powerful Stuff* in Memphis, Kim Wilson stopped by Wilkerson Sound Studios on Park Avenue, where the city's only nationally syndicated radio program, *Pulsebeat—The Voice of the Heartland,* was being

recorded. *Pulsebeat* had two weekly programs: a thirty-minute country music show and a sixty-minute blues show that was produced in
association with KFFA in Helena, Arkansas, the originator of the legendary *King Biscuit Time*.

Beginning in 1941, by broadcasting live blues every day at noon,
King Biscuit Time did for the blues what the *Grand Ole Opry* did for
country music. The most famous musician associated with the show
was Sonny Boy Williamson (his real name was Rice Miller), who performed on a regular basis for many years.

The show was actually Sonny Boy's idea, created after he went to
the station's white owner in 1941 and asked him to produce a blues
show. The owner told him that he would be happy to air a blues
show if Sonny Boy could find a sponsor for it. He sent Sonny Boy
over to talk to Max Moore, the owner of Interstate Grocery.

Moore, whose grocery had its own brand of flour called King
Biscuit Flour, was very interested in Sonny Boy's idea. He told Sonny
Boy that he would sponsor the show if Sonny Boy would allow him
to put his image on his brand of cornmeal, which he would market
as Sonny Boy Corn Meal. Thus was born KFFA's *King Biscuit Time*.

One of Sonny Boy's regular listeners in Mississippi was Riley
Ben King, who later changed his professional name to B. B. King.
All the time he was growing up in Mississippi, *King Biscuit Time*
was his main source of entertainment. "We would be in the fields
and we would go home for lunch," King later recalled. "We hurried so we would be there when 12:15 came so we could catch the
King Biscuit program. I heard them so long, it seemed like I really
knew them."

During its long run, *King Biscuit Time* only had two announcers—
Hugh Smith and Sunshine Sonny Payne. When *Pulsebeat* joined
forces with KFFA to re-create the blues show for a national audience,
Payne was still an announcer for the show and became a regular part
of the new show, which targeted both blues and AOR formats at
radio stations from New York to Texas.

A diminutive man who was more reserved than his big, booming
radio voice would indicate, Payne knew as much about the Delta
blues as anyone living. It was the sort of knowledge that came from
personal experience, not books. He and his boss, station owner Jim

Howe, spent most of their adult lives spreading the blues gospel because they felt it was important.

When Kim Wilson walked into Wilkerson Studio to record an interview, he was greeted by Payne and *Pulsebeat* announcers George Hays and Kim Spangler. A fourth announcer, Henry Nelson, was not present, but he was there in spirit. Nelson had a day job across town as an announcer at the 100,000-watt FM-100.

Skip Wilkerson, who engineered all the programs, had many years' experience in radio production. He didn't say much, but when he did speak it was usually to argue a point about the programming. Unfortunately he died of a heart attack a little more than a year after the interview with Kim Wilson took place. He was only fifty years of age.

Kim was in a noticeably good mood when he arrived. Whatever was happening over at Ardent obviously met with his approval. He was interviewed by George Hays, who began with a question about *Tuff Enuff*.

HAYS: Kim, what was it about the *Tuff Enuff* album that made it popular? Was it the message of the songs or its rhythm and blues feel?

WILSON: Well, it certainly wasn't the message of the songs. [laughs] "Our songs don't have much of a message. I think it was the sound. The song was a little different as far as the hook-type thing, but I think it was basically the sound. You get a catchy lyric and a catchy hook, people are going to go for it.

HAYS: With the success of that album, how has your audience changed over the years?

WILSON: [laughs] A little younger, a little whiter.

HAYS: You've played a lot of dates at Antone's in Austin. What have you learned about the blues audiences at Antone's?

WILSON: Well, it's just a joint, you know. Places really don't change, the joints don't change much, the people who go to them. It's a college town, so there're a lot of college kids. But a lot of locals come in and regulars, and when you walk into a place that you know has blues music, that's what you expect to hear. That's what happens every night. The nice thing about a joint is you never know what's going to happen. It's just a surprise. You might know a lot of the people who come in there, but lots of times something totally unexpected will go on and, I'm not saying it's always good, but most of the time it is.

HAYS: You enjoy playing clubs?

WILSON: I do. I do enjoy playing clubs. I enjoy playing every facet of it. I love playing, you know, arenas. I love playing theaters, all the way down to clubs. Really, I have the best of all worlds. I can go on one of the T-Birds tours and go out and play huge places and tour with people like Bob Segar and Eric Clapton, and I can come home and walk down to the corner bar. I've got a harmonica behind every cash register in town.

HAYS: What about the blues festivals that have sprung up all over the country? What do you think about the audiences?

WILSON: Well, naturally you love to see people attracted to the music. It's really great because the people who don't know what it is and come out of curiosity usually go away with a feeling of, wow, I never knew that was there. Once it bites you, you're hooked. What better than to be hooked on than music. It's a great thing. The New Orleans festivals are the ones that stick out in my mind the most. They do such a great job down there with it and you can see everybody you want to see, even in a lifetime, there.

We had our own night on a riverboat one year and we had Katie Webster, Dr. John, Roomful of Blues horns, Duke Robillard, Rockin' Sidney, it was just amazing . . . and Bonnie Raitt was on that also. On the fairgrounds, you know, they stagger it so you can see everybody, one right after the other, plus the food is fantastic. It's the ideal setting for blues and rhythm and blues and Cajun music.

HAYS: As a fan, you almost get mad at the organizers because you want to see someone here, and it's a quarter of a mile away to see someone else.

WILSON: Yeah, sometimes they can't make it exactly how you want it. But you just have to give up fifteen minutes of one person to go see the other one.

HAYS: With your recent success, you can draw the huge crowds to the auditoriums and get the bigger dates touring and you're also in demand in the studio. Do you see any danger spending time in the studio and the big gigs, as opposed to the clubs?

WILSON: I can really do anything I want to. I mean, I really have the best of all worlds. I don't worry about that kind of stuff. I can go work with Albert Collins or Jimmy Rogers or Pinetop Perkins or Buddy Guy. Anytime I'm off, that's what I do, if I'm not writing or collaborating with someone. Like here in Memphis, I go write with David Porter. I've got so many things I can do. It's never boring. It's always satisfying. Life isn't going to always be perfectly satisfying, no matter what you do. So what you have to do for yourself is make sure that you surround yourself with all the situations that you can to create an atmosphere for yourself.

HAYS: You recorded the *Hot Number* project and your current project here in Memphis. Why?

WILSON: It seemed like the thing to do. Memphis has got that soul fallout and we wanted to get a little on us. There are a lot of people around here to hang with. Ardent Studios is a very comfortable place to record. It's just got everything we want. We didn't have to go to Los Angeles or New York, which is all right for some people, but we aren't that cosmo.

HAYS: You didn't use horns on *Tuff Enuff,* but you did on your most recent album. Are you going to use horns on your current album.

WILSON: No. This time we aren't even going to use keyboards [the T-birds later changed their minds and added a keyboard]. It's going to be a real back-to-basics kind of thing for us. I'm real happy with it so far. I'm going to knock on wood if I can find any. [knock, knock] I really like it. I think it's going to be. . . . I'm not going to say anything. I'm not going to say anything. No predictions. But I will say this: That I'm happy about it. I always enjoy being in the studio and seeing things materialize. Especially to see one of your own songs that started with an idea and can go into something that you can touch. It's just a fantastic thing. It's like having a child.

HAYS: You mentioned earlier about writing with David Porter. Do you enjoy writing with other folks or would you rather sit down by yourself?

WILSON: Normally, I would rather sit down by myself. But I have a few partners out there that I love to work with. I just met David and I'm really having a great time doing things with him. Another guy that I write with and share ideas with is Nick Lowe, who I think is one of the most talented guys out there. He just has ideas bubbling out of him. I like to surround myself with people like that. You find that people like that need someone like yourself to bounce off of as well.

HAYS: What about the songs that you wrote for the new album?

WILSON: I've only got three, but one I wrote with David and David's got a couple. Three of them are by Jerry Williams out of Fort Worth. That leaves one, which is "Raining in My Heart," by Slim Harpo.

HAYS: With the advent of music videos, do you take that into account when you sit down to write a song or record a song?

WILSON: No. I don't even think about that. My songs have so many pictures involved, there's no way you could think of a video. That's one complaint I really have about music videos. A lot of them out there, 90 percent, would be nothing without a picture. You have to have a song and take it from there. Make any picture you want to from there. But if you've just got a picture and that's it, it's usually just a picture and a drum machine. It's a drag. I don't like watching them. I especially don't like listening to them.

HAYS: You received some flack recently from a New York music writer who seemed to be disappointed that the T-Birds are white and not black. What's your response to criticism like that?

WILSON: I think he can kiss my sweet little white butt. I know the guy you're talking about and he trashes everybody there, everybody who plays this music who happens to be Caucasian. The guy's got a tin ear and somebody's probably messed with his sister. I don't know. He's a minority. All I've got to say to the guy is ask Muddy Waters or Albert Collins what they think about me. I think they have better credentials.

The last article he wrote was about Stevie and a couple of other people. We weren't mentioned, thank God. He even got a few names wrong. Writers are there to create controversy and everybody wants to hear negative news. That's the only reason I can think of that they would do it. They like to take nasty shots at people so that the readers can see the reaction from the other side. It's just the usual sensationalistic journalism. Irresponsible. Totally abusing freedom of the press and the guy shouldn't even be working. I would say he had to do a lot of favors to keep his job.

HAYS: Blues has gotten a lot of attention this past year than it has in a long time. Do you have any idea why?

WILSON: [pauses, his thoughts still on the previous question] I got caught up in that last question. [apologetic laughter] Ask me again.

HAYS: [repeats the question]

WILSON: Well, I think it's reached the radio. I'd like to think that we had at lot to do with it. Of course, there are a lot of people out there—Robert Cray [for example], and when you see people like Albert Collins in movies, everyone is doing their part. All the labels like Alligator and Antone's and Black Top, at least they bring it to the forefront.

I know most of them are honest. It's just that the media has taken over on it and they haven't dropped the ball on it. It's a great thing to see. It has created a lot of opportunities for people who don't have opportunities. People like Pinetop Perkins. They get mentioned in articles all over the word. But I have would have to say, [the biggest impact is] the fact that it has gotten attention from radio.

At the end of the show, Kim was asked the question that all guests are asked: What song would you like to hear?

Kim laughed. "How 'bout 'Mannish Boy' by Muddy Waters?"

Later that day, back at Ardent Studios, the T-Birds returned to the business at hand: recording an album that they hoped would compare favorably with *Tuff Enuff*. There were reports that the friction between Kim and Jimmie escalated in the studio, but Preston Hubbard later said he had no memory of that.

"Jimmie and Kim, it was one of those things—they were so close, like brothers, that it was a love–hate situation," Preston said. "Both guys would get in fistfights, drink, and the next day it would be, 'I love you, man.' It's possible [they got into fights in the studio in Memphis] but I don't remember it. I saw plenty of that stuff [other times] but it never went deep. The first time we saw Jimmie and Kim get in a fight was in the really early days and I was in Roomful." Preston started laughing just thinking about it. "It freaked us out. It was like, Holy shit!"

Preston said that he was having a rough time with drugs when they were making *Powerful Stuff*. "I was kicking dope, but I still went in every day and did it," he said. "The drill with the Thunderbirds is that we would go into the studio pretty prepared, because we would rehearse at home first and work out the kinks. We did that with every record. We didn't go in there and write or work a song up. We were prepared. I just remember that it was comfortable and fun. Sometimes Joe Walsh was there in the next studio, so it was always fun and relaxed. It wasn't like we were on a timetable and [had to] hammer this shit out. We were prepared. We would get the rhythm tracks fast, sometimes in one take."

Fran Christina felt the same way. "It is one of my favorite places to record," he said. "There was always something going on. It was barbecue or Joe Walsh lining the studio with toilet paper and going out in the evening and seeing Duck Dunn and Steve Cropper. It was always a party."

While they were in Memphis, Fran was asked to be in a video with Jerry Lee Lewis. "They almost burned me up," he laughed. "They had these giant flash pots in the back shooting up flames. A couple of times, they had a tight shot of just me and Jerry Lee in the picture and no one was on the stage and they kept shooting off those giant flames. It was like being in hell with Jerry Lee. The place was all smoky and hot and he would be like playing away and he would turn around and look at me and he'd look like the devil himself and I'd get these chills and my hair would stand on end."

By 1988 it was apparent that the struggling Memphis music community was headed for trouble. Studios such as Ardent and Memphis Sound Productions were booked solid with out-of-town artists such as R.E.M., the Replacements, and George Thorogood and the Delaware Destroyers, who had heard about the revitalization effort and flocked to the city to tap into the music scene. But local artists, the people who were supposed to benefit the most from a musical rebirth, were often ignored and told to wait their turn.

Bob Pittman's QMI Music, which had signed two local artists to recording contracts and raised the expectations of everyone, ran into trouble after its first album, recorded by rocker Jimmy Davis, failed to get off the ground because of an ongoing dispute with the distributor.

Ever hopeful, Davis recorded a second album for QMI, but it was never released because QMI went out of business before it could be marketed. Pittman went on to better things, eventually becoming a top executive at AOL Time Warner, but Davis never saw his dreams come true. "We had spent a year making the [first] record and then went through the process of getting it out—and all of a sudden it was over," said Davis. "Part of me says that's the business, and I know it is, but, yeah, I got a raw deal."

On top of all the failed business ventures, individual musicians such as Jerry Lee Lewis, who had a home in Memphis and one in Nesbit, Mississippi, just south of Memphis, experienced financial problems. The Internal Revenue Service seized Lewis's possessions in a dispute over more than $3.7 million in back taxes.

While his wife, Kerrie, wrangled with IRS officials, Lewis set up residence in Ireland, where he said people knew how to treat musicians. Before the IRS could sell Lewis's property, Kerrie got an injunction to inspect them to locate items that belonged to their six-year-old son, Lee. It was all worked out eventually, and Lewis was given an opportunity to pay off the back taxes, but the episode served as a reminder of the sometimes quarrelsome nature of success in the music business.

Ironically, Memphis artists who were finding success were doing it in arenas far beyond the city limits. Jimi Jamison, lead singer for Survivor, belonged to that group. Survivor, which had scored big with "Eye of the Tiger" before Jamison joined the group, toured eight months out of the year, which meant that Jamison was able to spend four months a year in Memphis with his wife and his son, James Michael.

"You think, Boy, once I get that record it's going to be nothing but great," Jamison told *Nine-O-One* in 1988. "But once you get there, there's always another step. You always want to take it a little further. No matter how much money you make, you always want more. It's always something."

Chips Moman's Three Alarm Studio, the centerpiece of the city's revitalization effort, knew that "it's always something" feeling all too well. *Class of '55* had been a huge public relations success but a sales disappointment, sending America Records into a tailspin from which it never recovered. Moman's second Memphis album, Bobby Womack's *Womagic*, failed to make a dent on the charts that were top-heavy with female pop divas such as Janet Jackson, Cyndi Lauper, and Tina Turner. His third album, the Ringo Starr session, was blocked from ever being released. His fourth album, Willie Nelson's *What a Wonderful World*, was recorded in Texas but mixed at Three Alarm; it was beautifully produced and recorded, similar in concept to Nelson's heralded *Stardust* album, but for some reason it never caught on with country radio.

Over a two-year period, Moman had recorded with Johnny Cash, Roy Orbison, Carl Perkins, Jerry Lee Lewis, Bobby Womack, Ringo Starr, and Willie Nelson, yet he had little to show for his efforts: a failed record label, a string of lawsuits related to his recording ventures, and press coverage that went from adulation to outright hostility. His intentions had been nothing but good, yet, for some reason, it all went awry.

In 1989, the city's only daily newspaper, the *Commercial Appeal*, published a story under the headline "Songs of Greeting to Moman Are Grumbles Three Years Later," which recounted his difficulties in the city. Coming to Moman's defense in the article was Ardent owner John Fry. "Perhaps the biggest problem we have in Memphis has been the failure of people to understand that this is a music community but not a music capital," said Fry. "There was no way Chips Moman or anyone else coming in was going to change that, and anyone who thought he could was foolish."

Frustrated over news stories like that—and in disbelief over the run of bad luck he experienced in Memphis—Moman gave up on his dream of seeing a Memphis music revival and returned to Nashville, where he built a studio on a farm several miles from town and focused on recording new artists. Later he moved to his home state of Georgia.

With Moman's departure, Memphis music started unraveling—just as it did when he left in the early 1970s. Some believe that a voodoo curse is associated with Memphis music, a black magic spell that dooms those who dare to make music in the city.

Those who believe in the curse point to Elvis Presley, Otis Redding, and Al Jackson, all of whom died unexpectedly under mysterious circumstances—and they talk about the tragedies that affected Jerry Lee Lewis, with the deaths of two wives and a son, and Roy Orbison, with the death of his wife in a motorcycle accident and the death of two of his three children in a horrific house fire. If that is not enough to convince the doubters, they whisper the names of the artists who recorded hit records in Memphis, only to see their careers wither on the vine.

Among those not believing in the Memphis curse were the Vaughan brothers—hearty, no-nonsense Texans who didn't believe in black magic. Attracted to the Memphis vibe, the dark and some-times brilliant history of the birthing place for blues and rock 'n' roll, they strode into the city like guitar slingers on a mission from God, determined to beat the odds.

As a rejuvenated Stevie Ray Vaughan toured with a full schedule, his label, Epic Records, underwent an upheaval as the Japanese-owned Sony Corporation purchased CBS Records. Fearing that Stevie might get lost in the shuffle—it had been three years since he released a new studio album—Alex Hodges made a presentation to the new executives in May 1988 in an effort to refocus positive atten-tion on his client.

With all the negative publicity about Stevie's drug addiction and public breakdown in London, Hodges thought that the con-servative Japanese ownership might cut his client loose. In his pre-sentation, he stressed the steady sales maintained by his client and the Grammys and Handys that he had been awarded. Reaction to his presentation was positive, putting Hodges's fears to rest, but no additional funds were earmarked, as he had hoped, for the promo-tion of Stevie's next album.

As time approached to go into the studio again, Stevie hunkered down with songwriting partner Doyle Bramhall to come up with some new tunes. He was finding terrific new riffs on his guitar, but he was having a difficult time coming up with the right words, which was why he needed Bramhall.

It was a critical time for Stevie. He and the band had never recorded an album sober, and everyone was watching him closely to see if he would be able to deliver without the aid of mind-altering drugs.

There was also the question of what to do about Stevie's executive producer John Hammond, who had been ill in recent months. Hammond had been listed as the executive producer on all three of Stevie's studio albums, which meant that he handled the details of production and oversaw, in a general way, the artistic direction of the work. The actual producer for all three albums had been Stevie himself and engineer Richard Mullen.

With Hammond ill, that arrangement was no longer possible. Clearly Stevie would require an experienced producer in the studio with him for the next album, someone who would hold his feet to the fire. The stakes were too high to roll the dice on Stevie's ability to produce his own album.

Stevie's management and record label wanted a producer who had worked with guitarists and knew his way around a sound console. The person they all agreed on was Memphis producer Jim Gaines, who had produced and engineered Carlos Santana's records for ten years. He also was known for his work with Steve Miller and Huey Lewis.

"They were looking for somebody that was like a producer/engineer," explained Gaines. "Stevie and Carlos did a show together in California and he mentioned it to Carlos and he said, 'You might want to consider Jim—he does all of my work for me.' That was how the initial thing came up. They looked at five or six people, then I went down to Los Angeles and interviewed one day and had a meeting with them. I know they met with some other people as well, but I got the phone call saying that I had the job."

Actually, there was heated debate over who should be the producer. The record label wanted someone other than Gaines, an individual who reportedly had a drug problem, but Stevie and his management preferred Gaines, not just because of his heralded work with Santana but because he had never done drugs.

With the new album scheduled to be recorded at New York's Power Station, Gaines flew to New York in January 1989 and sat in on the band's rehearsals. When they felt they had the songs down to their satisfaction, they went to the Power Station to begin work on the album. Unfortunately Stevie was unhappy with the sound. They were there three days without recording a note. "Stevie didn't feel the room could give him what he wanted for his guitar amps," said Gaines, "so I made the decision to get out of there if we weren't going to record, because it was too expensive."

Four months earlier, Gaines had worked on a project for a Canadian band at Kiva Studios in Memphis. Owned by former American Records investor Gary Belz and Joe Walsh, the studio was located in midtown on Rayner Street, between Bellevue and McLean, in the general vicinity of the old Stax Records building.

Kiva went through several name changes over the years. First owned by Sam the Sham, who had a big hit in 1965 with "Wooly Bully," it had several subsequent owners, including the Bar-Kays, before Belz and Walsh bought it in 1987. It changed names again in 1996, when Walsh dropped out and was replaced by Isaac Tigrett, one of Belz's longtime friends. They changed the name of the studio from Kiva (named after one of Belz's grandmothers) to the House of Blues Studio, a name that Tigrett had chosen for a chain of nightclubs and hotels, and a number of Internet and multimedia ventures.

With the situation at the Power Station deteriorating by the minute, Gaines called Kiva and asked if Stevie and the band could have some time to test the studio. Kiva said they could have one week. "I actually got to the studio before Stevie and kinda' messed around with the room," said Gaines. "If that didn't work, we were going to Los Angeles. It was that simple. We knew we could find rooms there. It's not that the Power Station is not a great studio. The room they had us in was just a little too small for us."

When Stevie and Double Trouble arrived in Memphis, they knew they didn't want to leave, so any talk of moving on to Los Angeles was stifled. Besides, Kiva had two studios available. They spent a few days testing out the rooms and then hired the entire studio to record the album.

Gaines had never worked with ten amps, all cranked up at once, so that was the first problem he had to overcome. "I had recorded three or four amps at once with Carlos Santana—we always had a couple of Marshalls and a Fender Twin or something—but I said, 'Ten amps is a lot,' but I'm like a renegade engineer and I'll do anything," Gaines explained. "I said I had no problem trying it as long as we have a room big enough to handle it all. When you're talking about ten amps, you're talking about some heavy, heavy sounds."

No sooner had Gaines adjusted to the reality of ten amps, than he was informed that Stevie wanted to record his solos live. "That was another big, big job," said Gaines. "The whole track has to come down at once with the solos. Most guys would have said, 'Are you kidding me?' I said, 'Let's try it. We won't know until we try it,' and that's what we did."

The more complicated the session shaped up to be, the more concerned Gaines became about how it would have to be recorded. "I realized that I needed digital," he said. "But I'm a little opposed to digital. They're opposed to digital. We're all opposed to digital. I set up a twenty-four-track analog machine and a thirty-two-track digital machine side by side and had them go out into the studio and jam for a few minutes.

"I said, 'Just go out and play and I'm going to play the tracks back to you and whatever you choose is what we'll go with.' But I really want to go digital because I really need those extra eight tracks. I played it back for them and they chose the digital. I thought, 'Thank God!' Because I really needed those extra tracks."

Once Gaines got all ten of Stevie's amps set up, he encountered another problem. For some reason, every time he cranked up Stevie's amps there was a loud hum. He spent three days trying to track down the source. At one point, he asked the city to shut down the power grid for the entire block so that he could experiment with various solutions. Explained Gaines: "It wasn't so much an AC hum; it was more like a magnetic hum." He built a lead box, thinking it would help, but that didn't solve the problem.

"Finally I called some friends in New York and they said they had had that same problem," said Gaines. "They said, what you have to do is build a grid. Sort of like the copper grids that a lot of studios had. It's like a mesh that breaks up the magnetic flow. So I bought some chicken wire and some conduit and built what looked like a batting cage and put Stevie inside of it."

Gaines's infamous "chicken coop," which was about seven feet wide and five feet deep, knocked down about 60 percent of the hum, enough for them to proceed with the session. Stevie didn't mind playing inside a chicken coop. He thought it was cool.

Technical problems weren't the only considerations going into the session. Stevie and Tommy Shannon feared making an album while they were sober. They weren't sure what to expect because they had never recorded without drugs and alcohol.

"Stevie and I were scared to death," Shannon told the *Dallas Observer*. "We were terrified because we had never done anything like that in our lives. We were thinking, 'What if we just don't have it anymore?'"

Stevie told *Guitar World* much the same thing: "I thought the hardest thing would be, 'Oh, God, now I'm straight—can I still play?' But that had nothing to do with it. The hardest part is trying to keep things in perspective. I found out that the biggest problem that I had was self-centeredness and ego. That's really what my addiction seems to boil down to. To keep that part of myself under control while everybody's telling you how great you are is quite a task."

Gaines booked both sound rooms in the studio for three months and turned the smaller room into a maintenance facility. He covered up the console with a tarp and set the talk-back feature so that he could communicate with the guitar and amp technicians directly from his console in the other studio.

Shortly after they got started, Gaines came down with the flu and, to the surprise of Stevie and the band, asked Richard Mullen, the engineer on their previous album, to come to Memphis and sub for him while he was ill. It was a shocking thing for Gaines to do because Mullen and Stevie were involved in a lawsuit and management had wanted Gaines to *replace* Mullen. "They were a little hesitant because Richard had sued them over some royalties or something," explained Gaines. "But I said, 'I've got to get somebody that understands you guys.' I was so sick that I was in bed."

When Gaines returned to the studio after his illness, he found that everything had proceeded as planned. Mullen was sent back to Texas and Gaines resumed his place behind the console. After getting the studio set up the way he and Stevie wanted, Gaines turned his attention to the material they would be recording.

Stevie and Double Trouble showed up with seven or eight songs, and new material continued to arrive on a daily basis. "I woke up one morning with someone knocking on my door with a bunch of songs in his hands," said Gaines. "A week later, another guy showed up with songs in his hands. Just knocked on my door in the hotel. Songs constantly arrived as we were cutting. There are three or four tracks that we cut that Stevie never put vocals on."

The album title, *In Step,* was a reference to Stevie's devotion to the twelve-step program he was following to maintain his sobriety. "Wall of Denial," which Stevie cowrote with Bramhall, addressed his former problems with alcohol and drugs. Gaines said it was one of his favorite songs. "It took a while to record," he said. "It's pretty obvious what it's about. 'Wall of Denial' put the cap on the whole story. 'This is what I've been through and this is where I'm going.' Plus, it's just a cool song. We cut it two or three times, but we got it."

The album ended up being a mix of songs cowritten by Stevie ("Wall of Denial," "Scratch-N-Sniff," "The House Is Rockin'," and "Tightrope"), one song written by Shannon, Layton, Wynans, and others ("Crossfire"), several traditional blues covers (Willie Dixon's "Let Me Love You Baby," Buddy Guy's "Leave My Girl Alone," and Howlin' Wolf's "Love Me Darlin' "), and two instrumentals, one of which ("Travis Walk") Stevie recorded on the spot in a sudden burst of musical energy.

"Crossfire," the song written by the band members, was a tough song for Stevie to warm up to. It reminded him of something that Junior Walker would do. "I thought it was a neat song, but . . . I was uncomfortable playing it," Stevie told *Guitar World.* "I didn't know what to play! And it was hard to admit that I didn't know what to play. I just said, 'This is weird!' . . . But then I came to grips with it. I had to let the band carry the riff, and it has taken me a while to learn to let the band carry what they're going to carry anyway, you know? I don't have to be all over everything to make it work."

Gaines first heard about the second instrumental, "Riviera Paradise," when he met Stevie in New York. "I had a list of songs, and I said, 'What about this "Riviera Paradise" thing?'" Gaines later recalled. "Stevie said, 'Don't worry about that. It's just a little instrumental that we do. We don't really need to rehearse. We'll just cut it one night and it'll be fine.' So I didn't get to hear it in rehearsal. I didn't know how long it was. I didn't know anything about it."

They had been in the studio about a month, when Stevie said he wanted to play "Riviera Paradise." He told Gaines that it was a song that he wanted to cut late at night. "It's a late night feel, and we'll turn the lights down," said Stevie.

"Okay," said Gaines, checking his machine. It showed six or seven minutes of tape left. "How long is the song?"

About four minutes," answered Stevie. "We'll just take a whack at it and if we get it, we get it."

"Riviera Paradise" is a slow-moving jazz number with fluid, bluesy guitar licks that grab the listener from the first note, a powerful song with symphonic depth. Gaines immediately was pulled into the song, which has a mesmerizing effect on the listener.

Gaines was grooving on the song, thinking, "Holy shit—this is a special cut," when he looked over at the tape counter, then he was thinking, "Oh no, it's still going and I only have a minute and half of tape left."

Suddenly Gaines became very concerned. "I'm running around in the control room like a chicken with its head cut off, trying to get someone's attention," he said. "Stevie has his back to me and he has his lights turned down. Chris and the rest of them were all out in the studio with their heads down.

"Finally, Chris looks up at me and I give him this que sign that I'm running out of tape. I make this circle sign and cut, cut, cut . . . and I'm thinking, oh shit, I'm not going to get it on tape. Stevie looked up for just a second and Chris gave him the cut sign and I swear to you, the last note hit and I had about three seconds and the tape went plump.

"It was the only take that we ever did. We tried it a couple of other times, but it never came close. The solo is live. The only thing I fixed on it was Reese's part on the keyboard. We added some rainstick to it. It was a magic moment."

Standing outside the rear entrance of the Peabody Hotel, Stevie Ray Vaughan—or Ben T. Fender, as he was registered at the hotel—seemed out of place beside a doorman dressed to the hilt and a constant stream of southern Yuppies (or Slurpies as they are affectionately known to the blues pickers a block away on Beale Street) entering the hotel oblivious to his presence. Or maybe it was just that he seemed incomplete. True, he had on his trademark Tex-Mex parka and his traditional black, wide-brimmed hat. But something was missing.

It was not until Stevie got into the car with the *Pulsebeat* producer, who had come to pick him up for an interview, that it was apparent what was missing. It was his *guitar!* Without it, his hands seemed curiously empty, unsure of themselves.

As they got under way, Stevie asked if he could smoke. The producer didn't ordinarily allow people to smoke in his car, but Stevie asked in such a genuinely *nice* way that he didn't have the heart to say no. He didn't play with his cigarette the way most guitar players do. He held onto it quietly, almost passively, the way someone might hold onto an electric appliance that had not yet been plugged in.

They circled around onto Beale Street so that Stevie could see the home of the blues. There wasn't much to see, really. Several new restaurants and bars. Some small shops. A number of buildings under renovation.

"This is where it all started," the producer said.

"Man," Stevie said, taking it all in, his eyes dancing from one side of the street to the other as white clouds of smoke wafted about his face. They made the block and got on Union, driving past Sun Studio as they went east toward Wilkerson Sound Studios, where the interview was scheduled to take place.

"I can just feel it," said Stevie.

"Feel what?" asked the producer.

"The Memphis thing," he said. "I can feel it all around me. It just comes up out of the ground or something. There's just something about the place."

Stevie turned and gazed out the window, puffing on his cigarette as he searched the passing landscape for some ghost of a memory. Not seeing anything of note, he turned back and said, "It's out there—you can't see it, maybe, but it's there."

When they arrived at the studio, Stevie greeted his interviewer, George Hays, warmly and agreed to record several promos before the interview began. He was handed a sheet of paper that contained several greetings for him to read. The first one read, "Hi, I'm Stevie Ray Vaughan. Don't go away. We'll be right back."

Stevie looked over the sheet, then leaned into the microphone. "Hi, I'm Stevie Ray Vaughan. Don't go right away." He doubled over with laughter. *"Don't go right away!"* he repeated. "Sometimes I can read and sometimes I can't."

Once the program began, Stevie grew more serious as the conversation shifted to his music.

HAYS: Stevie, the blues have had their ups and downs, but these days things are definitely on the upswing. What do you attribute that to?

SRV: Well, a lot of people have had the chance to listen to this music. As a result, with radio and with record companies giving it more of a chance and starting to listen to the people who know what they want to hear, as opposed to being told what they want to hear. A lot of open doors. A lot of people with the guts to get out and tell the record companies, this is what we play. If you don't believe it's worth listening to, put a record out and find out, you know. A lot of doors were opened for us that way and we've had the chance to open some doors for other people. It's a give and take kind of thing.

HAYS: Has there ever been a time in your career when you were sorry that you devoted so much to the blues?

SRV: No. [laughs] Never!

HAYS: In songwriting, are you able to write while you're touring, or do you need to set that time aside to write?

SRV: That's a difficult question to answer. Sometimes they come to you and you can't stop them and sometimes you can't get going. There have been times when in the back of the bus I could write and write and write, and there's been times, not so long ago, within the past few months actually, when I would start a song and not be able to finish it. I ended up . . . it was a fun thing to do . . . finding a need to collaborate with someone. Recently we did six songs together.

HAYS: What do you think are some of the biggest lessons that a blues player just starting out can learn from the masters?

SRV: Take your time. Feel what you play before you play it and then feel it while you play it. Play only what you really want to play. For me, one of the things that came easily, and I'm very fortunate, was that I learned early on that if I didn't really care about what I was going to play, if I didn't really like it, that I couldn't give it all that I had and it's going to sound that way. Money pays the bills, but it ain't the best thing in life. What we go through in life, that's really it.

HAYS: Have you ever been caught with a great idea for a song and didn't have a guitar handy?

SRV: Oh, yeah. First you wake up and rub your eyes and try to get into it. Sometimes it seems ideas come out of the blue. Sometimes it's what somebody says to you. Sometimes you can remember and sometimes you can't.

HAYS: How's *In Step* different from other albums you've done?

SRV: It's the first record we've done sober, for one thing. That's probably the biggest change in my life that's ever happened. As a result, there is more attention paid to what we're saying and how we say it. It's been a real exciting album for us. And we're looking forward to the things that go along with it.

HAYS: You are taking better care of yourself. . . .

SRV: Oh, yes.

HAYS: Why are musicians so hard on themselves?

SRV: Not only are there a lot of pressures, there's a lot of emotion and a lot of us are alcoholics and addicts. That condition is not only an art-related thing, it really is rampant through all forms of society. It's just that a lot of artists of different kinds are under pressure by needing to keep going and keeping up this expectation of being bigger than life. A lot of times you're expected . . . the show must go on and you take a snort of this or a big belt of that to keep going. It's not necessarily by any means a long-lasting solution. It just appears to be at first. Thank God that some of us have the chance to come around and see that and live through it, and some of us haven't. I'm just glad to be one of the fortunate ones.

HAYS: On your new album, what is the favorite cut for you and why?

SRV: Well, I don't have a favorite one. There's one on there that just came bursting out. We were at rehearsal, trying to decide what we wanted to put on the record, and we were at kind of a standstill. I had my guitar strapped on and I walked over to this corner in the rehearsal hall and all of a sudden it was like an explosion. I just felt like I had to play this thing! I had never heard it before. Had never thought of it before. Right now we're calling it "Travis Walk." It just came busting out. It came from me walking across this thing and I just remembered that I lived on Travis Street and it seemed like an appropriate title. But it came out with a Louisiana-type feel and it's got some influences from Lonnie Mack. It's just one of those get-it songs, you know.

HAYS: If there was one song off your new album that you could put in a time capsule to be opened up years from now, which one would it be?

SRV: One song, huh? Probably a song titled "Wall of Denial."

HAYS: What's it about?

SRV: It's about the facade that we put up to keep from seeing what we need to see, knowing that the truth is really what keeps us going—and we're never safe from it, but we're always safe in it.

HAYS: If you could bring back any musician that's passed away, who would you like to record an album with?

SRV: One?

HAYS: Or two.

SRV: Well, I would be afraid to leave one of them out. I would love to just *see* the Wolf. And if he wanted to hear me, then we might talk about recording. And, of course, I would love to play with Hendrix.

After the show, Stevie talked with Hays a few minutes. The announcer had recently lost his father and Stevie talked to him about how hard losing his father had been on him. Stevie made the ride back to the hotel without a cigarette. The questions had stimulated his imagination and he talked some more about his new album.

Later Stevie's publicist, Charles Comer, called the producer and told him that he had spoken to Stevie after the interview and he had told him how much he had enjoyed it. "Why wouldn't he?" Comer said. "Don't forget, you were involved with the blues, everything he was into."

Comer explained that when Stevie went to Memphis, Stevie asked Comer not to set up any interviews for him because he didn't want to be distracted from the album. He made an exception for the *Pulsebeat* interview, Comer said, because he believed in what the producer was trying to do with the program. It would prove to be the only interview Stevie did while recording the new album. Stevie was like that—loyal to the cause.

One day, while Stevie was at work on the album, Albert King strolled into Kiva Studios to hang out for a while. "They loved each other," said producer Jim Gaines, who went on to explain that King was typically unpredictable. "He said, 'Let me talk to Mr. High Hat Man' [Chris Layton]. Man, that part you're playing is all wrong'— Chris looks over at Stevie and it was like, 'What am I supposed to do here?'

"One afternoon he comes in and while he's sitting beside me, I get this phone call. 'Bon Jovi is in town and they want Stevie and Albert to sit in with them tonight.' I'm on the talk-back and Stevie's out in the studio. Albert turns around to me and says, 'Hey, Jim, are them Bon Jovis big?' I said, 'Yeah, you might want to go.' But he didn't. He went and played cards with some lady. Stevie went though."

For Gaines, the biggest challenge he faced was simply capturing Stevie being Stevie. "I have worked with some hot-shot guitar players and artists, so it wasn't my first endeavor with a major artist," he said. "The thing that made me want to do this is once you hear him playing out there, you want to do anything you can to capture it on tape. I'll stand on my head if I have to. I just want to get him captured on tape because he is the best at what he is doing. I'm not going to say he's the best guitar player in the world. I'm going to say that Stevie Ray was the best, ever, that I've ever met of what he is doing and what he is about. Hendrix was great at what he did. I'm working with Carlos Santana and he's the best at what he does. I'm a laid-back hillbilly. I'll do anything I can, just give me a minute to work it out. They gave me my minute and that was all I could ask."

Of course, not every day spent on the session was stress free. There were problems with the equipment. Amps blew out. Strings broke. And there were problems getting it down on tape. It was the first time Stevie ever had a producer hold his feet to the coals. Gaines has perfectionist tendencies and he surprised Stevie from time to time by demanding that he redo guitar parts and vocals.

"Stevie is a great guy—he has that big smile on his face and that handshake was like a blacksmith's—for a little guy, he had the strongest handshake I've ever seen—but being in a working environment, we had our tense moments sometimes," said Gaines. "When I'd say it's not good enough, we need to do it again, there were some tense moments, because up to that point, they had just gotten by with what they wanted to do. If they wanted to do one cut and call it quits, that was it because there was no one overseeing them."

Stevie had a love–hate relationship with his music. He loved playing live, performing for thousands of cheering fans, but he disliked studio work because it was so tedious and because it gave him no immediate feedback on his performance. That was especially true with his vocals, for if he made a mistake it was right there in front of him and everyone else to hear, with no crowd noise to mask the mistake. To help him keep his voice in shape, Stevie kept an assortment of Halls cough drops on the music stand in front of him, along with lemons and hot sauce.

"Stevie hated singing," said Gaines. "In order to get him ready to sing, you had to get him all emotionally wound up and calmed down at the same time. He would do a take and I would say, 'No man, we've got to do it again.' We had some confrontations. He would say, 'What do you mean it's not good enough?'

"So that's where we had to draw the line. On some days he'd go out there and start playing before the other guys got there and tear up half the amps. Then we had to stop and repair the amps. It really depended on his emotional status on that day.

"A lot of it had to do with what kind of situation he had with Janna. I remember sitting in the studio several days, not making a move until he talked to Janna. The band's going, 'Jim, why don't you make him go to work?' I'd say, 'Heh, you're his buddies, you make him work.' That was when he was sitting around waiting for his girlfriend to call because he's worried about her. There were some tense moments."

One night, during the second month of production, Stevie and Gaines went to the hotel bar after wrapping up at the studio. Stevie ordered a Coca-Cola and Gaines ordered a glass of orange juice. They talked for a while, unwinding from the stress of the studio; then at around 2:30 a.m. they got on the elevator to go to their rooms.

When the elevator door opened on their floor, Stevie asked Gaines if he was tired. Gaines said no, so Stevie suggested that they sit down in the chairs at the elevator door and talk some more. He clearly had something troublesome on his mind.

"He started pouring out some stuff to me that I didn't want to hear," Gaines said. "This was personal stuff. Stuff that happened to him in the past and he just wanted to talk to somebody. So we talked for over an hour. Then I got up and said it was time to go to bed. I'm like one of those hug people and it's like give me a big hug and he hugged me and wouldn't let go. It freaked me right out. He needed someone to talk to that wasn't in the family, wasn't in the clique.

"Once we got done, it was like we were brothers or cousins. He kept holding onto me and holding onto me, and he's a pretty strong little guy. It kind of freaked me out. Shit, man, I just heard a bunch of stuff that I really shouldn't be hearing. Family secret stuff. There were things with him and his dad and his brother. There was stuff that went down, man, that they didn't have a great happy home life. When he started telling me this stuff, I thought, I don't want to know. We had good times and we had those spiritual times and that was a spiritual time for me."

Once they finished up in Memphis, they all went to Los Angeles to do the mixes and vocal overdubs. That could have taken place in Memphis, but after three months in the city, Stevie was ready to work in a studio that was closer to Janna.

While Gaines was putting the finishing touches on the album, he was interviewed by a guitar magazine. Shortly before the article came out, Charles Comer called him and told him that he was going to be unhappy with the story because the writer had gotten him confused with another Memphis producer, Terry Manning.

Later the editor called Gaines and apologized. The error was discovered too late to make any changes, so when it was published all of Gaines's quotes and good work on the album were attributed to Terry Manning, who had nothing to do with the album.

"The editor said he didn't know how that could happen," Gaines said. "I said I didn't know how it could happen either."

CHAPTER 6

Tragedy Strikes as Stevie Falls *In Step*

S TEVIE'S NEW ALBUM, *In Step*, hit the sales racks in July 1989, only three months after production was wrapped. The cover pictured Stevie wearing a woolen poncho and his trademark hat, head bowed so that his face could not be seen, kneeling on the floor with a National steel guitar propped on his knee.

In Step was greeted with steady sales, but it never managed to climb past number 33 on the album charts. America's interests that summer went more along the lines of Madonna's "Express Yourself" and Milli Vanilli's "Girl I'm Gonna Miss You." Nonetheless, critics called *In Step* Stevie's best album ever.

To his surprise, producer Jim Gaines received a telephone call from the record company asking if he could cut down the nearly nine-minute "Riviera Paradise" to three or four minutes so that they could release it to jazz stations.

"I tried to cut it down—and they tried—but there was no way to cut it because of the way it is structured and because it is always moving to another level," said Gaines. "I spent an entire day trying and then told them that I couldn't."

Of the ten songs on the album, "Crossfire," the only tune that Stevie was slow to warm to, "Tightrope," and "Wall of Denial" received the most attention, with the instrumental, "Travis Walk," also attracting notice.

Stevie started promoting the album in Dallas by appearing on the nationally syndicated radio show *Rockline*. He did the interview from the studios of Q-102, a station that had played his music from the very beginning of his career. He delighted listeners by picking up a guitar and launching into "Travis Walk" on live radio.

From Dallas, Stevie and Double Trouble began a ten-day concert tour that took them from Dallas to Los Angeles to Philadelphia and then back to Dallas, with enough stops in between for them to perform every night.

The following month, Stevie performed at the highly publicized Who reunion tour, on the same bill with the Fabulous Thunderbirds. After the show, Stevie told Jimmie that he was ready to do the Vaughan Brothers album that they had talked about for a long time. Jimmie was noncommittal, probably because he wanted his own star to rise higher before they did a joint venture. He was the big brother, yet music writers kept asking him if he was proud of his successful BIG brother. He was not comfortable living in Stevie's shadow. He just needed a little time, that's all.

As the summer wore on, Epic Records decided to pair its two hottest guitar slingers, Stevie Ray Vaughan and Jeff Beck, in a tour they named "The Fire Meets the Fury," a reference to the guitarists' incendiary personas.

Ten years older than Stevie, the British-born Beck had begun his career in the mid-1960s with the Yardbirds, a group that also featured Eric Clapton and Robert Plant in its many incarnations. The band's biggest hit was "For Your Love," which peaked at number 11 in June 1965, behind the Byrds' "Mr. Tambourine Man," the Beatles' "Ticket to Ride," the Beach Boys' "Help Me, Rhonda," and Elvis Presley's "Crying in the Chapel." It was an incredible summer for music, with the Rolling Stones' "(I Can't Get No) Satisfaction," Beau Brummels's "Just a Little," and Sir Douglas Quintet's "She's about a Mover" rounding out the Top 20.

Beck left the Yardbirds in 1966 to pursue a solo career, but after recording a series of singles that failed to attract attention, he formed a new band called the Jeff Beck Group. It featured future Rolling Stones guitarist Ron Wood on bass and Mickey Waller on drums, and included an up-and-coming singer named Rod Stewart. They released two successful albums, *Truth* and *Beck-Ola*, but then broke up in 1968 on the eve of a scheduled performance at Woodstock.

From 1968 to 1989, when he went on tour with Stevie, Beck released a series of well-received albums, one of which, *Blow by Blow*, sold more than 2 million copies and peaked at number 3 on the album charts. But for the past ten years he had kept a relatively low profile, avoiding concert appearances entirely.

With the release of *Jeff Beck's Guitar Shop* in 1989, Beck was ready to hit the road again. The record label and the guitarists' managers spent weeks going back and forth over who would be the headliner. Stevie was probably hotter at the moment (many of his fans were too young to have heard of the British guitarist), but Beck had been a star longer and had a more loyal fan base. In the end, they flipped a coin to determine who would be the headliner, with the order reversing for each performance.

"It's a tour that will make guitar nuts howl with joy and whammy bars whine in terror," wrote Ted Drozdowski in *Rolling Stone*. Stevie told the magazine that Jeff Beck was one of his heroes. "A lot of my ideas came from hearing people like Jeff Beck and Eric Clapton, who I first heard at the same time I started listening to Howlin' Wolf and Muddy Waters and all those guys when I was real young," he said. "I think every guitar player who came up in Texas played 'Jeff's Boogie.'" Beck told the magazine that he was "eager to get into this with Stevie."

They rehearsed in Minneapolis, Minnesota, before kicking off the tour in that city's Northrop Memorial Auditorium; then they moved on to Chicago, where they paid a surprise visit to Buddy Guy's new club, Legends. In all, they hit more than thirty cities.

After their performance at the USF Sundome in Tampa, Florida, Katherine Bessette interviewed Beck backstage for *Outer Shell*. He told her that he was torn between opening for Aerosmith or touring with Stevie, and decided on the latter since he would be the headliner half the time.

Beck said that his management told him that touring with Stevie would be "much better for [him] than the stockings and suspender belt–type girlie audiences," and he agreed with them. But he added, "I love Aerosmith just as much, but we thought this is a smaller deal, and it's a good way to start re-touring."

At a stop in Cleveland, Ohio, the two men talked to *Guitar Player* about their mutual admiration. Said Stevie to Beck: "A lot of your tones are really tones of meat and fingers. It's a lot warmer, and a lot more personal. . . . Getting to know this guy is one of the coolest things about the tour for me . . . it's been a lifelong thing to me, listening to you, man, and for me it's an honor to be out here with you now."

Responded Beck: "I think Stevie's playing state-of-the-art blues at the moment. There's no one who has that tone, and the venom that goes with it."

The high point of the tour for everyone was the final show, a 19,000-seat sellout at New York's Madison Square Garden. "Jeff Beck still knows how to make notes sound hard-won-sustained and ethereal, then nasty or tearing—and when he stays with the melody . . . it sounds as heartfelt as any vocal could make it," observed the *New York Times* reviewer, who was clearly more taken with Beck than with Stevie. After the show, Stevie walked across the street to the Beacon Theater and sat in with Jimmie and the Fabulous Thunderbirds on their last encore of the evening.

Not long after that performance, Jimmie followed Stevie's lead and checked himself into a rehab program. When he emerged, he told Stevie that he was ready to make that album they had been talking about for years.

For the first time, they were at the same place in their lives. Drawn together by the death of their father, they felt grateful for the second chance they had both been given concerning their addictions. Both felt somewhat burned out on the music they had been playing, Jimmie more so than Stevie—and they were both eager for new experiences.

In February 1990, Stevie and Double Trouble won a Grammy for *In Step* in the Best Contemporary Blues Album category. Stevie attended the ceremony and, flashing his broadest smile, was obviously excited about the award. Before leaving the stage, he told the audience, "Now we've got to get Buddy Guy one of these!"

Jimmie Vaughan's entry into a rehab program totally changed his perspective about his family. When he emerged, he felt a need to be close to them and to communicate more effectively with them, which is why, after Stevie's tour ended, he was ready to go into the studio with his younger brother.

The first thing they had to decide was where to record the album. Stevie's last album had been recorded in Memphis and so had the Fabulous Thunderbird's previous two albums, so it seemed only right that they return to the birthplace of the blues and the home of rock 'n' roll. They talked about whether to record at Kiva or at Ardent and decided on the latter, for no reason in particular other than that Jimmie liked it there and had never recorded at Kiva. What was the point in being a big brother if you couldn't throw your weight around a little?

The next task was to agree on a producer and an engineer. Since Jimmie got to pick the studio, Stevie chose the producer—Nile Rodgers, with whom he had worked on David Bowie's very successful *Let's Dance* album. For engineer, Jimmie countered with an Ardent staffer, John Hampton.

Rodgers had begun his music career in the mid-1970s by working as a studio musician in New York studios. One day the guitarist and several other studio musicians decided to record a disco song that they had written titled "Dance, Dance, Dance (Yowsah, Yowsah, Yowsah)." An Atlantic Records executive loved the song and signed the musicians to record an entire album. They named themselves Chic.

"Dance, Dance, Dance" went on to become a Top 10 hit. The following year Chic scored with another disco tune titled "Everybody Dance." By 1983 Chic had outlived the disco craze and had no reason to exist. When the band broke up, Rodgers returned to studio work, which is what he was doing when Stevie Vaughan met him.

Rodgers wanted to record the Vaughan brothers' album at Skyline Studios, his production headquarters in New York, but neither brother liked New York well enough to want to record there. Rodgers gave in to their demand to record in Memphis, with the understanding that he could take the tapes to New York and do the postproduction at Skyline, where he had a Synclavier (a sophisticated computer with a piano keyboard that allows its operator to manipulate a track in myriad ways).

With the studio, the producer, and the engineer in place, the Vaughan brothers tackled the very ticklish task of what to do about a band. The T-Birds and Double Trouble were tight bands because everyone had learned to work together and to anticipate each other's moves. Stevie and Jimmie knew that they couldn't pick one rhythm section over the other—and using individual members from both groups made no sense—so they decided to allow Rodgers to put together a new band for them. He chose bassist Al Berry and drummer Larry Aberman, musicians who had never played with either brother.

Before heading out to Memphis, the brothers huddled in Dallas and Austin to select and rehearse songs. Stevie worked with his old friend Doyle Bramhall and came up with three songs: "Hard to Be," an old-style rock 'n' roll song to which they added horns; "Long Way from Home," a drum-driven song with a silly vocal introduction; and "Telephone Song," a traditional Texas shuffle that would be welcomed by Stevie's fans.

Jimmie and Stevie put together two instrumentals: "Hillbillies from Outerspace" and "Brothers," a bluesy slow song featuring Rockin' Sydney on accordion and a weird vocal shout that totally ruined the mood of the record. Jimmie contributed a third instrumental, "D/FW," an up-tempo song that started out with another inappropriate vocal.

The brothers collaborated with old friend Denny Freeman on "Baboom/Mama Said," a rhythm and blues number that featured a shout and answer but a minimum of lyrics. Rounding out their song selection was "White Boots," a Billy Swan composition, and what would prove to be the strongest song of the session, "Tick Tock," a slow song written by Jimmie, Rodgers, and Jerry Williams.

The first thing Stevie did when he arrived at Ardent Studios was line up his guitars, all thirty-one of them, according to engineer John

Hampton, who added good-naturedly, "but he always played the same stupid guitar."

Interviewed more than a decade after the session, Hampton provided valuable insight into how each song was recorded by focusing on one particular song, Billy Swan's "White Boots." The process began when Jimmie came in one day with a musical shard, a portion of the guitar lick that he envisioned for the song.

"We're all sitting there, playing Game Boy," recalls Hampton. "And while he's playing Game Boy, Jimmie sings a verse and plays the shard. Niles never looks up from his Game Boy; he just throws an arrangement together. He had brought with him the drummer and the bass player and this guy Rich Hilton [Rodgers's engineer at Skyline]—and Rich was key to all this. Rich is a superfocused anti-Nile Rodgers, the exact opposite of him. He starts saying, 'Rich, make me something out of this lick.'

"Then they'd make a B-section and a chorus, blah, blah, blah, and they would put it all into the computer. There was a drum machine and it would be Rich making out which chords went where. It was all recorded on a forty-eight-track Sony. Then, after the map was on the tape and Niles gave it his thumbs-up, we would start cutting the drummer, putting him down on it. If this guy was a fifteen-billionth of a second off the beat, Nile would stop and we would go back five bars and punch him in.

"It was not a continuous performance with the band; it was quite the opposite. First, there would be a scratch vocal for the song, then Nile would say, 'put a drum file here,' and then Larry would start playing drums to it and the scratch vocal would guide Larry to where he was in the song. That was the first time in my life to punch in drums."

Because Hampton is a drummer himself, he was dubious of Rodgers's penchant for "punching in" sample rhythms on the drum tracks. "I didn't trust any digital tape recorder to be as precise as I wanted them to be," said Hampton. "But, boy, that Sony machine was dead on and Nile showed me a few tricks, like to hit it right dead on the backbeat and you will get it because it actually punches in a tiny bit after it.

"After we had the drums, the bass player came in and laid down the bass part. Keep in mind, all we had at that point was a keyboard track mapping it out, and then a real drum track and Al came in and laid down a bass track. Then Nile, Stevie, or Jimmie would play it as a scratch guitar track, or Jimmie would lay down the real guitar track, depending on the song.

"On 'White Boots,' Jimmie stood in the control room and Nile spoon-fed him a little of this or that, not that he needed it. Once the guitar track was down, then Nile got an idea for a guitar track and he put down another guitar on the track and he went to Stevie and said, 'Stevie, do you want to put anything down'—and in this case, Stevie said, 'Naw, that's pretty cool.'"

Stevie and Jimmie arrived at the studio each day around 2:00 p.m. and worked until early morning. Rodgers was amazed at the difference he saw in Stevie. He had not seen him in years, not since he had been through rehab. "Stevie was always a loving guy, that part of him was no different," he told *Musician* magazine. "But he was more gentle now, and very focused. You could tell he found a different life when he gave up drugs. And his spirit was stronger than ever."

Hampton was equally impressed by Stevie's strong emotional state. "He was just beginning his clean act, you know what I mean?" said Hampton. "He was chewing tons of Nicoret gum. They would go to an AA meeting probably three times a day. We'd be in the middle of a guitar part and if Stevie got frustrated, he would turn everything off and say, 'Let's go to a meeting.' . . . I think Jimmie was starting to clean up then. Everyone was off the drugs and booze and if there was any weirdness there, it was just the frustration of [making a record].

"You know, even if you stop smoking, it drives you crazy. Rather than pick up a cigarette, you go to a meeting. If your nerves get rattled, instead of buying a bottle of booze, you go to a meeting. They would go around the corner, go to a meeting and come back feeling great. As the day wore on, you could feel the tension building, then Stevie would go to a meeting. They would sometimes come back from the meetings and sometimes they would call and say they were having too much fun and weren't going to work any more that day."

"Tick Tock," the most talked-about song on the album, was written by Jimmie one day while he was sitting on his porch playing his guitar. Well, Jimmie wrote part of it. The guitar part was there, but he couldn't seem to finish it. It took three of them—Jimmie, along with Rodgers and Jerry Williams—to fully flesh out the song and give it, through its lyrics, a world-peace anthem that had the dual role of addressing both Jimmie's and Stevie's troubled lives.

When the song was finished, it had a soulful, Memphis groove to it. Jimmie did the vocal introduction and Stevie did the main vocal. As they recorded it, Rodgers became emotional. "I just sat there with tears in my eyes, thinking, '[Stevie] doesn't even understand his power,'" he told *Musician*.

Contrary to press releases that accompanied the release of the album, Stevie and Jimmie did not participate in any type of dueling-guitar antics in Memphis while making the album. "They didn't do any playing together, handing each other guitars—at least not in my presence" said Hampton. "To be honest, that seems like some kind of spin that CBS put on it. Knowing Nile, that would be too out of control for him."

The Memphis sessions only lasted two weeks, after which Jimmie and Stevie took the tapes home to the Dallas Sound Lab, where they recorded two of the instrumentals, "Brothers" and "Hillbillies from Outerspace." For those tracks, Rich Hilton replaced Hampton as engineer. The drummer and bass player were also replaced.

"So I'm hanging out at home and I get this call," said T-Bird bassist Preston Hubbard. "They said, 'Hey, Preston, we need you to come to play. So I got in my car and drove up to Dallas."

Preston was surprised, to say the least, since Stevie and Jimmie had let everyone know that none of their band members would participate in the project. Feelings had been hurt. Sure, doing it without them made sense on paper, but it seemed almost heartless for the brothers to exclude *everyone* who had supported them along the way from such a long anticipated album.

To his surprise, he found Doyle Bramhall on drums, with both Jimmie and Stevie there ready to play live. They started at nine and finished both songs by eleven. "They were really passing the guitar back and forth," said Preston. "They were having a fucking ball. We were all in the same main room and they were having a great time. Stevie was just straight up, a wonderful guy. I don't remember ever having any kind of problem with him. In the studio, we just ran over the songs a couple of times and that was it. It was tracked. Three years later, American Express used 'Hillbillies from Outerspace' on a commercial with no voice-over and it was great."

When the session was over, Preston got in the car with his girlfriend, who had traveled with him, and drove back to Austin. From Dallas, the tapes traveled to Rodgers's studio in New York, where he settled down to work his magic in private.

"We got a whole lot done in the two weeks they were [in Memphis]," said Hampton. "We got all the tracks and the basic guitars. From there, it went to Niles's 'lab' and God knows what that is. Rich Hilton gave me the hint that it is a Synclavier-based system, which is why we had everything mapped out. You can feed it to the Synclavier and sample it and move it anywhere you want it. You could pick up something from the first chorus, if it was really good, and move it to the second chorus."

Hampton said the finished product was a little different from what they did in the studio. "All of a sudden, there would be a turnaround in the song," he explained. "We cut vocals here and how many ended up on the record, I couldn't tell you. All the basic rhythm guitars ended up on the record . . . [and] some of the stuff he did for scratch keyboards ended up on the record."

Years later, Rodgers told *Guitar Player* that he had indeed used his Synclavier to electronically edit the tapes. "Stevie loved that," he said. "He'd go out there and use the Synclavier himself, and I thought, 'Oh God—what have I done?'" Rodgers told the magazine that he felt he had failed to capture on tape what he and the brothers felt in their hearts. "I'm a little disappointed with myself. Something was developing, not only between Jimmie and Stevie and myself, but between all of the musicians involved. . . . I did the best job I could, but I never got to develop that relationship artistically to the next level."

After the session, Jimmie and Stevie didn't feel exhausted, the way they always had felt after finishing previous projects. On the contrary, they felt reinvigorated, as if they had experienced a rebirth of some kind. And they felt closer to each other.

"We've probably gotten closer making this record than we have been since were little kids at home," Stevie told VH1. "And, uh, I needed it, you know? I can honestly say I needed it." It was a sentiment that Jimmie echoed: "It was like we had gotten back together, and it was almost like we were at home. I had never seen him happier."

Flush with the success of the *Family Style* session, Jimmie returned to the grind of playing guitar for the Fabulous Thunderbirds. It was a grind for him because he no longer agreed with Kim Wilson about the direction the band should take.

The T-Birds had built their reputation on a retro style of playing that reflected the musical sensibilities of the 1950s, both blues and rock 'n' roll, but that no longer interested Jimmie. He wanted to take their music to the next level, whatever that happened to be. Did he really want to spend the rest of his life playing three-chord boogies in smoky bars for patrons who cared more about their drinks than the music?

Of course, his dissatisfaction with the band was about more than music. He viewed life differently after going through rehab. His priorities changed. He felt a new closeness to Stevie and to his mother. In his eyes, the T-Birds began to look more like a hindrance to personal growth than his salvation, which is the way he previously felt.

After leaving Memphis, Jimmie accompanied the T-Birds to the New Orleans Jazz and Heritage Festival, an event that they always loved to participate in. Then it was on to the T-Bird Riverfest in Austin, after which he told the band that he was leaving to pursue new opportunities with Stevie. Kim would be free to take the band in any direction that he chose.

No one in the band was really surprised. Fran Christina had seen it coming during their last tour of Australia. "I think he was just coming to grips with his problems and his habits, and decided it was time to straighten them out and he did," said Fran. "He's a brave, strong man for doing it."

In Jimmie's case, straightening out his problems involved making new friends and associates. Successfully completing rehab often radically alters friendships, causing the individual to see his old relationships in a negative light. Marriages that are built on addictive dysfunction have a difficult time surviving rehabilitation. For all practical purposes, the band was Jimmie's marriage. It was time to move on.

"I think he just burned out, man," said Preston Hubbard. "Like a lot of us did. We'd been out so long. You get to a point when you're kinda' fooling yourself. Stevie had gotten clean and Jimmie took heart and looked at that. He had founded the T-Birds with Kim and they had been out there so many years. . . . There was no huge fight. Jimmie said, 'I don't want to do this anymore. I want to get my life on track.' He was kind of killing himself toward the end. The immediate response to that was that everyone understood. No one tried to talk him out of it. There were no fights.

"Then there were three of us. We said, 'Okay, Jimmie is leaving the Thunderbirds. What do you guys want to do?' Everyone said, 'Let's go on.'"

With Jimmie gone, Kim and Fran called Roomful of Blues cofounder Duke Robillard and Kid Bangham, a hot guitarist out of Pennsylvania, and asked them to join the T-Birds. For Fran, who had begun his career with Robillard, it was a full-circle moment. Robillard had a thriving solo career at the time, but he put it aside to ramble with the T-Birds.

Epic Records was not thrilled with Jimmie's departure, but the record label gave the reorganized group a shot at another album. *Walk That Walk, Talk That Talk* was released in 1991 to generally good reviews, but it never did the sales that the *Tuff Enuff* album enjoyed. With Jimmie gone, Kim pushed the band more toward the soul side of the rhythm and blues spectrum.

The T-Birds toured relentlessly to promote the new album, but their efforts had little effect on sales. T-Birds fans wanted to hear the early hits, the ones that Jimmie had played on. When it became obvious that the album was going nowhere, the band focused on becoming a great touring band, traveling from coast to coast in the United States and all across Europe, where the blues still counted for something, even if it was more soul and rock 'n' roll than traditional blues.

By that time, Preston's drug use had gotten out of control and he tried to kick his addiction to methadone and heroin. "Through it all, my bass tech would keep a trash can in the wings for me to puke in," Preston wrote in "Into the Abyss." "I would need a stool to sit on for many performances, and Kim would call songs sans bass so that I could go backstage when necessary to lie down. It was a nightmare, but the boys hung through it all with me, sympathizing with my plight."

In 1992 the T-Birds returned to Memphis for the Beale Street Music Festival. They performed on the Delta stage sandwiched between Jon Butcher and Spyro Gyra. The festival was held on the banks of the Mississippi River in the shadow of the Memphis skyline.

There were three stages, with the Delta stage and the Blues stage catering to so-called smaller acts. The headliners, such as Albert King, Edgar Winter, Lynyrd Skynrd, Johnny Winter, and Gladys Knight were placed on the River stage. All three stages were kept up and running from late in the afternoon until early in the morning.

When the T-Birds were halfway through their set, Albert King cranked up his band, drawing people away from the Delta stage. It was King's last major performance in the city that had launched his career. Memphis had always run hot and cold for King. Born in Indianola, Mississippi, the same city that gave the world B. B. King, he grew up in the Mississippi and Arkansas Delta and reached the height of his popularity in the 1960s and early 1970s while recording for Stax Records in Memphis. After Stax crashed, he went more than ten years without attracting anything other than passing attention in Memphis. Now, at sixty-nine years of age, he was again the toast of Memphis.

Sadly, King never lived to see the year out. He died on December 21, 1992, in Memphis of a massive heart attack. The day of his funeral, radio station WDIA played nothing but his music, introducing a new generation to the sounds of "Laundromat Blues," "Cross Cut Saw," "I Walked All Night Long," and "I'll Play the Blues for You."

In some respects, Memphis music died along with Albert King. There were only a handful of people from the old days left in the city—Sun Records founder Sam Phillips was still there, but he had given up on music years ago. Jim Stewart and Estelle Axton still called Memphis home, but Estelle had not thought seriously about music since "Disco Duck." Jim continued to work with new acts, producing albums for the R&B charts; ex-Booker T. and the MGs bassist Duck Dunn remained in Memphis but went to Nashville whenever he wanted to record. In the wake of Chips Moman's departure, all hope of a Memphis music revival was seemingly sucked out of the city with tornadic velocity.

There were some victories in the early 1990s with hard-rock bands, including Tora Tora, Human Radio, Every Mother's Nightmare, and Roxy Blue (which was signed by Geffen Records and produced by Mike Clink, who worked with Motley Crue), but they were short-lived and all ended in failure.

"There have been many times when I've said, 'I can't take this any more,'" said Jimmy Davis, who saw his dreams crash with the failure of QMI Records. He told the *Commercial Appeal*, "None of the things that happened to us were our fault. We did everything we were supposed to do. I want to be paid, but that's not why I'm in this business. I'm in it because I love it."

Instead of being a city that unleashed great talent, Memphis recorded great talent that was attracted to the city because of its reputation as a historic music center. That proved to be a good thing for producers such as Willie Mitchell, Jim Gaines, Terry Manning, Jim Dickinson, Keith Sykes, Bobby Manuel, and John Hampton.

Recording studios such as Ardent and the House of Blues thrived, redefining Memphis music. From 1990 to 1994, Ardent recorded albums for Robert Cray, Lynyrd Skynyrd, the Jeff Healey Band, B. B. King, Albert Collins, the Allman Brothers, Steve Earle, the Gin Blossoms, the Spin Doctors, and of course ZZ Top, a band that continued to record its albums there in secrecy.

The Fabulous Thunderbirds never returned to Memphis to record, though Jimmie did. With the failure of *Walk That Walk, Talk That Talk*, Duke Robillard gave his notice in 1993 to return to his solo career. Preston Hubbard followed in March 1994, after the band did two weeks in Reno, Nevada. "It all came to a head one night backstage, with tempers flaring between Kim and me," Preston wrote in his memoir. "So I just said, 'fuck it,' and turned in my walking papers. Ten years—truly the end of an era."

By that point, Preston was spending half his time being sick and the other half high on heroin and cocaine. He went from five-star hotels to dirty junkie pads. Out of work, he turned to drug dealing to support himself and his habit. Eventually he was busted and ended up doing time in a Texas penitentiary.

Fran Christina stayed with the T-Birds several more years but then burned out, primarily because of the constant traveling. His last performance with the T-Birds was in Temple, Texas. "It was a giant arena and there were only about 350 people there," he said. "I thought, 'This is really not going out in style.' Someone had made a mistake on when the gig was going to be. It was my last gig and it was totally anticlimatic."

During the George W. Bush–Al Gore presidential campaign, he was tempted to go back out on the road by Bob Dylan who invited him to a concert in Newport. Said Fran: "I was looking out at the audience—me and my sister and Shawn Colvin and Al Gore—and we were listening to Bob and I looked out over the crowd of 20,000 people and I was getting hot to play and I looked back over the back of the stage and saw the buses. Dylan has asked me to join the band, but I just couldn't get back on that bus. That's when I knew my touring days were over."

Today he performs when he wants to, but he spends most of his time helping his wife, Julie Speed, further her blossoming career as a serious artist. About his days on the road with Jimmie, he says, "There was never a dull moment, I'll tell you. My biggest thrill about it was making the music and all the other stuff that went on between was just guys on the road having fun. We were just a family. We'd get crazy together. We'd get pissed off at each other. And, sometimes, we had to save each other's neck. . . . It was certainly the best time of my life."

With work on *Family Style* almost completed, except for minor overdubs, Stevie spent most of the summer on tour with Joe Cocker, awaiting the release of the album. Named the Power and Passion tour, it carried Stevie back over familiar ground, as they played large stadiums all across the country in cities that Stevie knew from his days of performing in small clubs—Dallas, Houston, Nashville, then up into the Northeast, with performances in New Jersey and New Hampshire, and back to the West Coast.

In Seattle a fan handed a crew member an envelope that contained a rubbing of Hendrix's headstone. When Stevie opened it and read it, chills spread all over him. He quickly handed the piece of paper to a roadie and ordered that it be destroyed. Fans had a weird sense of what made their heroes happy.

On August 22, 1990, Sony Records arranged a preview party in Dallas for *Family Style*. Stevie didn't attend because he and Janna had flown to Hawaii for a brief vacation before the final leg of the tour. Stevie had gone through a lot in the past year, but he felt he was ready to marry Janna. They made tentative plans and she agreed to be photographed in a white wedding gown for a Dallas magazine.

When Stevie and Janna returned, they went to New York, where she had modeling work lined up. Then Stevie left for Chicago, where he checked into the Four Seasons Hotel, using it as a base to venture out to dates in the Chicago area.

On August 24, Stevie and Double Trouble performed at the Kalamazoo County Fair. They arrived there after a long, tiresome ride in a van through more than one hundred miles of heavy traffic. But the audience was enthusiastic about the performance, and that seemed to take the edge off of the trip.

The following day, they piled into the same van for a trip to East Troy, Wisconsin, for a two-day booking with Eric Clapton at the Alpine Valley Music Theater. Also on the bill were Robert Cray with the Memphis Horns and surprise guests Jimmie Vaughan, Bonnie Raitt, and Jeff Healey, the blind Toronto guitarist who befriended Stevie in the late 1980s. At the end of the show, Clapton was joined on stage by Cray, Healey, Jimmie, and Stevie for an informal jam that kept the audience of more than 25,000 on its feet.

In Step producer Jim Gaines, who was working in Lake Geneva, about twenty minutes away from the venue, meant to attend that concert but got tied up with a recording project. "I was working at the Royal Studios with this Australian artist who got bored in Memphis," recalled Gaines. "I needed to do some vocals, so we went to Lake Geneva. That particular studio is hooked onto what used to be the Playboy Club up there. The studio is at the end of the hotel. They're trying to close the hotel down because of asbestos problems."

Gaines was all set to go to the second show on August 26, when he received a call from Santana. "He said, 'Please come to Chicago and mix my radio show they are doing at the World Theater outside of Chicago.' I said, 'All right. I'd just like to get back in time to see Stevie.' So I get there and there's no way I'm going to get back in time. . . . By the time I get through with Santana and hit rush-hour traffic, we don't get back until ten o'clock. I'm in my room, thinking, well, 'I'll just catch them later.'"

At the previous show, Stevie had made comments about the van ride to the venue and someone suggested that next time he should hitch a ride on one of the four helicopters that ferried performers from the Chicago hotel to Alpine Valley. On August 26, Stevie did just that and boarded a helicopter in Chicago for the ride out to the venue.

By all accounts, it was a spectacular show. Robert Cray and the Memphis Horns opened and were followed by Stevie and Double Trouble. They performed for nearly an hour, doing several songs from *In Step*, including "Wall of Denial" and "Riviera Paradise," along with earlier hits such as "Couldn't Stand the Weather" and "Pride and Joy." Also mixed in with his originals were several covers, including Stevie Wonder's "Superstition" and Jimi Hendrix's "Voodoo Chile."

"In a way, his tense, driving leads . . . seemed more an expression of flat-out celebration than of brooding anger or frustrated desire," wrote Mikal Gilmore for *Rolling Stone*. "It was as if Vaughan had played all the way through his blues and was not striving to find what sort of music one could create on the other side—in short, what might result when one takes a music of anguish and lust and transforms it into a music of hope and determination."

Eric Clapton followed Stevie and then invited Stevie and Jimmie back on stage, along with Cray and special guest Buddy Guy, to jam on the last song of the evening, "Sweet Home Chicago." Clapton was clearly the star of the show, but the respect he had for the other guitarists was transparent to everyone there. A fog had rolled into the valley during Clapton's performance, giving the arena a surreal appearance, especially in the low-lying areas away from the bright lights that surrounded the stage.

Each guitarist took a turn displaying his musical wares. Clapton was precise, his individual notes paced for maximum effectiveness. Cray was rhythmical, grouping his notes into grapelike clusters. Jimmie was low-down bluesy, going more for tone. Guy was primal, his notes sounding like an injured beast thrashing about in the forest.

Then there was Stevie, who played like a man possessed, high notes screaming though the mist. "It was Stevie's night, and I think anybody will tell you that," Jimmie later told VH1. "He was just amazing. . . . He was really happy all day."

After the show, Stevie hung around a while, talking to the other musicians, especially Clapton, with whom he hoped to perform soon at London's Royal Albert Hall, while Tommy Shannon grabbed one of the first helicopter flights back to the hotel. Usually Stevie liked to hang around and talk to the fans for a while, but this time he didn't; instead he voiced eagerness to get back to Chicago so that he could catch a flight to New York and be with Janna.

Stevie was told that one of the helicopters had three available seats. That sounded perfect to him, so he asked Jimmie and his wife, Connie, to accompany him. Just before liftoff, however, Stevie was told that the other seats were taken by Bobby Brooks, Clapton's agent, Nigel Brown, Clapton's bodyguard, and Colin Smythe, Clapton's assistant tour manager. Stevie apologetically asked Jimmie if he minded if he took the only seat on that flight. Jimmie, not wanting to be separated from his wife, told him that was fine. He and Connie would just catch the next flight.

Stevie's Bell 260B Jet Ranger helicopter took off in dense fog at 12:40 a.m., veered off to one side, and then disappeared into the darkness. Right behind Stevie in another helicopter were Eric Clapton, his agent, Roger Forrester, and Buddy Guy, who expressed apprehension about flying in the fog.

When the time came for Jimmie and Connie, Chris Layton, and Jimmie's manager, Mark Proct to board, they were told that the incoming pilot did not want to land at Alpine Valley because of the fog. They were asked to make the short drive to Lake Geneva, so that the helicopter could pick them up there, as the pilot considered it safer for a nighttime landing.

Everyone involved with the show made it back to the hotel and went to bed, unaware that one of the helicopters had failed to return. The only people aware of a problem were officials with the Federal Aviation Administration, who had been notified that a downed helicopter was sending out an emergency radio beacon. Using satellite technology, they pinpointed the site of the radio beacon and ordered ground crews to visit the location at first light.

It was nearly 7:00 a.m. before sheriff's deputies arrived at the site and located the wreckage. Ironically, it was located on a three hundred-foot-high hill a short distance from where the helicopter had lifted off. From the looks of things, the helicopter had slammed into the hill at a high rate of speed. It must have happened so quickly that Stevie and the other passengers never knew what hit them. Their bodies were strewn across a two-hundred-foot slope spotted with Queen Anne's lace.

Jimmie and Eric Clapton both received calls shortly after seven o'clock, notifying them of the accident. Together, they took a limousine back to the resort to identify the bodies.

"I was responsible for escorting Eric Clapton and Jimmie Vaughan to the morgue to identify the bodies," Jim Wincek told Keri Leigh. "They were both visibly shaken, and although I am what you would call a fan, none of that mattered when I met them. . . . Luckily, the bodies were not burned or dismembered, and they were then transported back to Chicago by hearse to be put on a plane that took the bodies home."

Word of the accident spread quickly. Jim Gaines was asleep when he received a call from Chris Layton shortly after seven o'clock. "He said, Jim, Stevie's helicopter didn't show up last night and we don't know what happened." An hour or two later, he called back and said, "Well, they found him."

"I felt like somebody had kicked me in the stomach. I was in a daze. I was just a mess. I had been up there working for a week or two prior to them arriving. It was so foggy. I drove along just looking at the white lines to make sure I was on the road, that's how foggy it was. Chris told me they had wiped the bubble down three times before they could take off. I thought, man, why would he even do that?"

Fran Christina was in Nova Scotia on vacation when he heard the news. "My friend comes over and says, Eric Clapton went down in a crash," he said. "I thought, gee, Stevie was on that tour, I hope he's all right. When I got to a telephone, I found out that it was Stevie who went down."

Preston Hubbard was asleep when he received a telephone call from a friend, who told him that she had heard about the accident on the radio. "I was like what?" Preston said. "She said he was dead. Jimmie and Connie were supposed to be on that helicopter, but they got bumped. We could have lost both Vaughan brothers, which would have been unbelievable. It didn't really hit me until later, when I kept seeing the news and the tributes. I think everyone was kind of dead for a while. It was such a shock."

Stevie's body was flown back to Dallas the next day, August 27, the fourth anniversary of Big Jim's death. Stevie's body was taken to Laurel Land Memorial Park in Oak Cliff, and the funeral and interment took place on August 31. Newspaper reporters estimated that more than three thousand mourners gathered outside the chapel, while family and friends mourned privately inside.

Attending the funeral were an assortment of friends and fellow musicians, including Stevie Wonder, the three members of ZZ Top (Billy Gibbons, Dusty Hill, and Frank Beard), Dr. John, Buddy Guy, Jeff Healy, Bonnie Raitt, Nile Rodgers, Ringo Starr, Jackson Browne, Kim Wilson, Fran Christina, and others. Among the pallbearers were Chris Layton, Tommy Shannon, Reese Wynans, and his manager, Alex Hodges.

Nile Rodgers eulogized Stevie by talking about "Tick Tock," the song he had produced for the *Family Style* album. "In the song, 'Tick Tock,' he sings the refrain, 'Remember,'" Rodgers said, according to Bill Milkowski of *Guitar World*. "What Stevie was trying to tell all of us was, 'Remember my music. Remember how important music is to all of us. And just remember that it's a gift.' Stevie was truly touched by the hand of God. He had a powerful gift."

Fran Christina flew in from Nova Scotia for the service. "What can you say about a funeral," he said. "There were a great bunch of people there. Stevie Wonder, just breaking into 'Amazing Grace.' It was pretty sad. He was just getting back on track, just getting over the hump and he was feeling good about himself again and his music started to have more coherence. It was such a shame. *He was ready to roll!*"

Stevie was laid to rest in the Laurel Land Cemetery next to his father, Jimmie Lee Vaughan, a World War II navy veteran. It was in a section of the cemetery reserved for veterans; Stevie was not a veteran, of course, but he qualified for burial there because of his father's military service.

Charles Comer, who had been with Stevie for nine years, said he had never seen him happier than he was that summer. "He was looking forward to his birthday on October 3 and to October 13, which would have been four years without a drink or a drug . . . and he was going to marry his girlfriend, Janna," said Comer. "He said to me, 'I've been given a second chance in life and not many people get a second chance.'"

Comer's voice was alternately filled with anguish over the loss of his friend and with joy over news he had received that day that *In Step* had zoomed to number 14 with a bullet on the Billboard charts. "We've never been higher then thirty-one in our lives. It's selling fantastically. We'll be at 750,000 by next month." He said he knew that that news would make Stevie smile, wherever he was.

Back in Memphis, Stevie's death reverberated with the same sense of disbelief and grief that was evident in Dallas and Austin. Memphis music writer Brown Burnett had just left an AA meeting when he learned of Stevie's death. "I recalled the day that I interviewed him and what he was saying," said Burnett. "Stevie Ray Vaughan was trying to tell *me* something to help me get sober. He knew I had a problem and he was doing what they call '12 stepping' me, spreading the message of sobriety . . . but since I was 'in the disease' at the time, I didn't get it.

"I couldn't hold back tears when I first heard about his death. I thought about how many people he touched, particularly me during the interview I did with him, and the people he still touches not only with his music, but with his sobriety. That part of his legacy lives on, along with his music.

"In an AA meeting the next day I told a story about how a prominent person, I didn't mention a name, shared his story with me once when I was drinking and how it took me years, and his death, for me to 'get it.' When Stevie was talking to me, I kept wondering, 'Why does he just keep telling me about this?' When I heard of his death, I 'got it.' He was trying to help me save my life."

In its obituary, *People* magazine wrote that Stevie was a "sad new addition to a series of similar air-crash tragedies" that involved musicians, but was "far more than a sad statistic." The magazine told of how Stevie had gone to Buddy Guy's assistance when he opened his Chicago nightclub. "Stevie is the best friend I've ever had, the best guitarist I ever heard and the best person anyone will ever want to know," Guy told the magazine. "He will be missed a lot."

CHAPTER 7

Do You Get the Blues?

WITHIN A PERIOD of months, thirty-nine-year-old Jimmie Vaughan had lost his band and his brother. He began withdrawing almost immediately from everyone around him, except for his mother, Martha. "I talked to him on the phone," said Preston Hubbard, who did not attend the funeral. "But I don't think I saw him until about five years later. He was devastated."

Jimmie became a recluse immediately after the funeral and probably would have remained disconnected from everyone outside his immediate family were it not for two unstoppable forces in his life: The release of *Family Style*, the album that he had recorded with Stevie, and the fact that Stevie did not leave a will directing how his estate should be handled.

Family Style was released slightly less than a month after Stevie's fatal accident. The album went to the Top 10 on the album charts, the highest either of the brothers had ever charted for an album. Of course, the album's extraordinary success was due to the publicity that Stevie's death had received in the national media. The album went on to receive two Grammys—one for Best Contemporary Blues Album, and the other for Best Rock Instrumental Performance (for "D/FW").

As a musician, Jimmie had lived most of his life for the moment, just as Stevie had done, immune to the daily responsibilities of adulthood. With Stevie's death, Jimmie was thrust into a position of responsibility that he had never anticipated. Since Stevie had not prepared a will, lawyers advised Jimmie and Martha to petition the probate court for an order naming them coexecutors of his estate. Stevie's fiancée, Janna Lapidus, was unceremoniously bumped out of the picture.

As part of the proceedings, the probate court inventoried Stevie's estate. He owned no real property, so the assessment centered on stock, savings, and royalties: fifty shares of nonvoting capital stock and fifty shares of voting capital stock in Stevie Ray Vaughan and Double Trouble, Inc. (valued at $6,612.50); sole stock ownership of Ray Vaughan Music, Inc. (valued at $17,048); bank accounts at City National Bank in Los Angeles, California, which contained $92,673.57; a certificate of deposit valued at $25,474.23; one 1975 Chevrolet Caprice valued at $1,000; audio and video recordings valued at $20,000; personal effects, including clothing and jewelry, valued at $20,000; thirty-four guitars valued at $28,450; speakers and amplifiers valued at $29,950; and song royalties valued at $300,000.

Once Jimmie and Martha were appointed coexecutors, they fired Stevie's manager, Alex Hodges, thus depriving him of any future earnings from Stevie's songs and recordings. Jimmie's manager, Mark Proct, was put in charge of looking after Stevie's music business affairs (he was eventually replaced by Cory L. Moore, a California-born promoter who once was involved with the Ringling Bros. circus).

Janna made several claims on the estate, but Jimmie and Martha turned them all down. She was asked to turn in the car that Stevie had leased for her and to vacate the condominium that she shared with him. Some people thought that she got a raw deal, especially in view of the love and devotion that she had provided to Stevie at a very critical time in his life.

Jimmie made a few personal appearances over the next couple of years—he went to Eric Clapton's annual Royal Albert Hall concert in February 1991, the one that Stevie had wanted to attend—but he backed away from his own career to oversee the details of Stevie's posthumous career, a sound business decision since Stevie earned more dead than Jimmie could have earned on his own.

When he wasn't overseeing the estate, Jimmie spent his time reconditioning old cars, which he entered in car shows, and listening to unreleased recordings that Stevie had made but rejected as substandard.

Jimmie and Martha ended up selling Stevie's song catalog to Sony Music for a substantial amount but retained artistic control over what was released. While they were sorting out the affairs of the estate, Jimmie and Martha filed a lawsuit against Omniflight Helicopters of Dallas alleging that the company was negligent in allowing an unqualified pilot to fly the helicopter and that the pilot was negligent for taking off in the dark in a dense fog.

Families of the other deceased passengers also filed lawsuits against the company. Omniflight reached a settlement in 1992 with the families of two of the crash victims, paying them more than $2 million, but the lawsuit filed by Jimmie and Martha dragged on until 1995, when the company settled with them for an undisclosed amount.

Tommy Shannon and Chris Layton knew that they would continue to benefit financially from the music that they had recorded with Stevie, especially from songs they had cowritten with him. Unlike Jimmie, who was busy with the paperwork of Stevie's death, they had little to do on a day-to-day basis.

Chris rented a rehearsal room at the Austin Rehearsal Complex, where he went early each morning to play his drums. One night he dreamed that he was there with Tommy—it was just the two of them there playing drums and bass—when the door opened and they saw Stevie peeking around the corner. Chris asked him what he was doing there. In the dream, which Chris related to Craig Lee Hopkins, Stevie entered the room and showed them a little bottle that seemed to contain a powder.

"I guess it was some old, leftover drug-related idea or something," Chris later recalled. "I didn't want to spoil the dream by saying that . . . and he walked in and picked up a guitar, and we played for a while. I remember it was really emotional, because I woke up and I was crying."

While they were playing, Stevie suddenly stopped and laid his guitar down and started for the door. Chris asked him where he was going. "That's it," Stevie told Chris in his dream. "My time's up. I gotta go."

Chris dreamed a lot in the months following Stevie's death. He didn't mind because he liked the dreams better than he liked real life. Tommy Shannon was in pretty much the same shape. "We had gone through hell together holding hands, and then we got a new life," he told the *Austin Chronicle*. "His death shook the faith I had, crumbled it. Then I realized that real faith was accepting death as a part of life."

It took a while for either Tommy or Chris to play again after Stevie's death. "I got to where I'd go out and listen to a band a little bit, and they'd ask me to sit in," Tommy told the *Dallas Observer*. "I found out it made me feel better to just get up there and play. It wasn't Stevie, which was a letdown because nobody can do what Stevie did. But . . . I started enjoying it and I noticed that it makes me feel better to play, so I started playing more and that started helping me more."

Several years later, when asked about performing without Stevie, Tommy told *USA Today* that Stevie was a tough act to follow. "Of course, most guitar players can't come close, which isn't to say there aren't guitar players we love playing with. Stevie spoiled us, because he had such intensity and fire."

Jimmie's next record project bore Stevie Ray Vaughan's name, *The Sky Is Crying*. He spent almost an entire year going through his brother's discarded recordings to find the material for the album. He quickly discovered that many of the recordings had been rejected for a reason—they were often incomplete segments, with botched guitar parts or rhythm tracks that were pocked with mistakes.

"When they were putting together *The Sky Is Crying*, Jimmie's manager called me and said, 'Man, we're looking for material that is left over from the *[In Step]* session, but we can find only a couple of things,'" said producer Jim Gaines. "I said, 'Man I recorded a whole bunch of stuff. I don't know what happened to it.' I said, 'Have you gone through all the tapes? There should be some instrumental stuff left.'

"They never found it. The tapes went back to Los Angeles because we were working on them in Los Angeles. I have an idea who has them, but I don't know if I want to mention any names at this point. All I can say is that management got the tapes before the record company [got them]. I think there are still some pieces and parts sitting around somewhere."

Most of Stevie's tracks were too long anyway, so that gave Jimmie an opportunity to edit them down, cutting out the substandard material while saving the good stuff and combining it with tracks from separate recordings. *The Sky Is Crying* is not so much a product of Stevie's passion as it is a quilt of his musical explorations.

When the album was released in October 1991, it debuted at number 10 on the *Billboard* album charts. Within three months it was certified platinum and went on to sell more than 1.5 million copies. It also did well at the 1992 Grammys, winning for Best Contemporary Blues Recording and Best Blues Instrumental (for "Little Wing," a Jimi Hendrix classic that was recorded during the session for *Couldn't Stand the Weather*).

Jimmie followed up *The Sky Is Crying* with *In the Beginning*, an album of live material that was recorded during a radio broadcast. Since it was done before Tommy Shannon joined the band, it features Jackie Newhouse on bass, a fact that some music purists found offensive, especially since Stevie had an opportunity to do something with the material and chose not to do so.

Newhouse ended up suing Jimmie and Martha for not compensating him for his efforts on the album. They reached a settlement after two years of negotiations. Unhappy with the release of the album was Chesley Millikin, one of Stevie's former managers. "He never wanted to have it released," he told Bill Crawford for the *Austin Chronicle*. "That tape was only released for one reason—greed."

Jimmie came under considerable criticism for the manner in which he packaged Stevie's old material. "Every time the label puts something out on Stevie, there's somebody going, 'Here we go.'" Jimmie told the *Austin Chronicle*. "They like to say stuff like [grave robbing]. . . . When you lose somebody you love, you want to put that somewhere, keep it close but get on with your life. But it's in my face every day. People loved Stevie, and they loved his music and so did I. . . . I didn't ask for that job. It just came to me. What would you do? Say no? No, you fight. That's what I did, and I still get shit for it."

After several years of dealing with Stevie's estate, Jimmie decided in 1993 to record an album of his own. He had learned a lot on the road with the T-Birds and while administering Stevie's estate, most importantly, that artists who write their own songs earn considerably more money than artists who do not.

By the time Jimmie went into the studio to record *Strange Pleasure*, he had written or cowritten enough songs to fill the album. The title song was an instrumental (one of two on the album) that featured just Jimmie and Dr. John on piano. It is an excellent song, simple yet layered with pauses and creative changes of pace. "Tilt A Whirl," the other instrumental, is a jazzy number that features a wailing sax. Jimmie was unselfish while recording the song, sharing the spotlight with the organ and sax.

The album has a definite New Orleans feel to it, although most of it was recorded in New York. That's probably because Jimmie collaborated with Dr. John on two songs and featured his piano work and vocals on other songs.

Nile Rodgers produced all the tracks on the album, except for one. For "Hey-Yeah," Jimmie returned to Memphis and produced the song himself, with John Hampton as the engineer. "I think he just needed one more song," says Hampton. "Just kind of made it up on the spot. It was this magic two-day session. Everything we did, we loved. That was the first time me and Jimmie worked by ourselves without anyone else."

Jimmie was inexorably drawn to Memphis, not just because it was where he and Stevie had enjoyed the happiest moments of their adult lives. They were attracted to the city itself. "I could always go to Memphis and pretend that I was part of that big, rich tradition," Jimmie told *Billboard*. "I'm a big fan of all the great blues and soul records from the 1960s and before. It's just endless, and it's very inspiring. When you go there, you plug into that."

On *Strange Pleasure*, for the first time, Jimmie was required to sing. He initially toyed with the idea of hiring someone to do the vocals but was persuaded that he would not be accepted as a solo artist if all he did was play the guitar.

"They told me, 'You have to sing,'" he explained to the *Arizona Republic.* "And I said, 'Well, I don't sing.' And they said, 'You have to.'"

Jimmie did remarkably well with his vocals. His voice doesn't reflect the passion or depth that Stevie put into his vocals, but he proved to be surprisingly good at steeping his inexperienced voice in nuance. He sings in the same way he plays: never giving too much but always providing just enough.

Given a choice between going for power or mood, he will invariably go for mood. He also makes liberal use of backing vocals. Another interesting characteristic of Jimmie's songs is that almost all of them fade out. He learned how to sing but didn't learn how to end a song.

The odd thing about *Strange Pleasure* is not that Jimmie sang on the album, or that he couldn't figure out how to end any of his songs, but rather that his solos were better than they were on any of his albums with the Fabulous Thunderbirds. "Don't Cha Know" features some superb guitar work, as does "Love the World," one of the songs he cowrote with Dr. John.

When *Strange Pleasure* was released, many critics were stunned. It debuted at number 1 on the *Billboard* Heatseeker Chart and garnered enthusiastic reviews from critics who seemed shocked that he could sing (why hadn't the T-Birds brought that side of him out?) and surprised that his solo guitar style was different from anything he displayed with the T-Birds or in his only album with Stevie, *Family Style.* Musically, Jimmie was full of surprises.

After the release of *Strange Pleasure*, Jimmie returned to the comforting seclusion that had enveloped him after Stevie's death. He no longer had the fire inside him to make music, at least not for public consumption.

For four years—four *long* years, his fans would say—he performed infrequently and recorded only on the album of Stevie's friend Doyle Bramhall. That project, *Bird Nest on the Ground*, was released in 1997, as was another Stevie Ray Vaughan project, *Live at Carnegie*, which featured live recordings from his appearance at the famed concert hall. Those two albums were a bright spot in an otherwise depressing year.

Keith Ferguson, the bass player who had toured with the T-Birds in the early years, died unexpectedly in April. The last years of his life were difficult for many reasons. In a 1996 story for the *Dallas Observer* headlined "Beautiful Loser," he came across as eccentric and detached from the music mainstream. He told writer Josh Friedman that he didn't receive enough royalties from his early work with the T-Birds to buy cigarettes. "I got a big check the other day— $3.22—from BMI," he said. "People tell you you're important, but apparently not important enough to give you money you've earned."

Jimmie never commented publicly about Ferguson's death, but it must have caused him to have a restless night or two, considering all the days and nights that he had spent on the road with him.

During those "lost" years, when music was something he did for his brother and not for himself, it was Jimmie's interest in classic and custom-built cars that gave him the most enjoyment. His first custom hot rod was a 1951 Chevy Fleetline. Over the years, he added a 1963 Buick Riviera and a 1961 Cadillac Coupe DeVille to his collection. "I don't play golf, so cars are my hobby," he once explained in a press release. "I was into cars as soon as I was old enough to walk. I built lots of models when I was a teenager. It's not like transportation. It's art you can drive to the store."

The DeVille was a gift from his mother, though it started out as something else. On a trip to visit his mother in Dallas, he picked up a copy of a local car magazine and saw a classic DeVille advertisement that attracted his attention. He took his mother with him to the auto show to see the car and borrowed the money from her to purchase it. Several days later, after he had driven the car back to Austin, she called and asked him how he liked his Christmas present. It was the best gift she could think of to buy him.

Several years later, he painted the car and entered it in the Roadster Show. Since most of the equipment on the car didn't work, he decided to refurbish it. He installed a massive 500-cubic-inch engine, along with El Dorado bucket seats. Then he had a backseat custom made to match the bucket seats. "Then we took the dash out and chromed the whole thing," he told Jamie O'Shea for *Juxtapoz*. "We did a ton of shit to it, but it still looks like a Cadillac—a dream Cadillac."

By 1998 Jimmie was eager to return to the recording studio, this time for an album titled *Out There*. Four of the ten songs—"The Ironic Twist," "Astral Projection Blues, "Motor Head Baby," and "Little Son, Big Sun"—were recorded in Memphis, which by 1998 had become more of a museum than a talent factory, though talent still flocked to the city to record at Ardent and the House of Blues.

All of the Memphis songs were produced by Jimmie and John Hampton, who also served as engineer. "The Ironic Twist," named after his DeVille Cadillac, is an instrumental that uses a tenor sax to get that gritty juke joint sound popularized by the Bill Black Combo of Memphis. Deliberately reproducing the sound of a smoky night-club, it allows Jimmie to dip into his bag of dirty-blues licks.

"Motor Head Baby," with lyrics all about hot cars and sweet love, is a throwback to 1950s rock 'n' roll. It pairs a piano with a B3 organ and offers the easygoing pace that Jimmie loves to play solos alongside.

"Astral Projection Blues" is one of the few slow songs on the album. Jimmie never quite brings off the vocal, but he gets credit for trying to stretch his limited range. Dr. John plays vibes and piano on the track and provides much needed flavoring. "Little Son, Big Sun" is an instrumental on which Jimmie plays both rhythm and lead guitar. It's a decent song but offers no real fireworks.

One of the main things that distinguished *Out There* was Jimmie's decision to allow the B3 organ player, Bill Willis, to play bass parts on the organ. The only track that had an actual bass guitar on it was "Kinky Woman," one of Jimmie's compositions.

"Like a King," which was written and produced by Nile Rodgers at his studio in New York, was the only song on the album not produced by Jimmie. Rodgers also played rhythm guitar on the track. Jimmie's solos were solid but the song never quite jelled.

Out There didn't achieve the level of sales that Sony needed to keep Jimmie on the roster, but it picked up a Grammy nomination for "Ironic Twist" in the Best Rock Instrumental category and it received good reviews. The *Boston Phoenix* felt that the album featured Jimmie's "best playing ever, bringing a rich-toned exuberance to the familiar trappings of rippling blues and shuffle beats, soul grooves, and vocal arrangements that tap the celestial richness of the glory of days of doo-wop."

The biggest problem that Jimmie ran into with his solo music was that there really wasn't much demand for retro explorations of the "glory days of doo-wop." Radio stations that played "oldies but goodies" wanted the real stuff, not retro versions, and pop stations wanted contemporary music recorded by much younger artists.

Compounding Jimmie's problem was the fact that he never had the young audience Stevie had been able to capture. Jimmie's audience was older, more inclined to want to hear him perform in a nightclub than in an arena. Statistically, his audience was the least likely to drive to the nearest record store to pick up his latest CD.

Out There came and went with barely a ripple in Jimmie's life. It hardly seemed worth the effort to write or cowrite eight songs and then record them, worrying over each and every note. Yet he felt compelled to continue doing it.

Jimmie's musical future lay in performing, not recording. In July 2000 he performed at the Republican National Convention in Philadelphia to show his support for Texas Governor George W. Bush. "When it comes to rhythm and blues, it doesn't get much better than Jimmie Vaughan," Bush told reporters. "And I'm honored to have him play at the Republican Convention."

Jimmie enjoyed rubbing shoulders with the political elite, but it was not something that necessarily endeared him to other musicians, most of whom viewed Bush's conservative politics with considerable skepticism.

The blues are without politics, but none of the original blues masters would have considered stepping foot into a Republican function. "I'm not a Republican. I'm not a Democrat, either," Jimmie told the *Austin Chronicle*. "I am Libertarian. Yes, I believe in the Constitution and the Bill of Rights. That's what I believe in. The rest is a bunch of horseshit."

Performing for the Bush family was old hat for Jimmie. Twelve years earlier, he had performed at the elder President George Bush's inauguration. It was an event that Jimmie described as "one of the most memorable gigs" of his life.

Taking up much of Jimmie's time in 1999 and 2000 was the work he did helping Sony prepare the three-disc box set, *SRV*, which was released in November 2000, about a decade after Stevie's death.

Since it contained forty-nine songs, many of them recorded live, it was a time-consuming venture for Jimmie.

More than half of the songs earmarked for the set were recorded live, an unusual mix for a box set. They came from a variety of sources, including performances on *Austin City Limits* and *MTV Unplugged*. Sales for the expensive box set were good and reviews were generally enthusiastic. Even though he was dead, Stevie Ray Vaughan still outsold his older brother, a distinction that was not lost on Jimmie.

With two solo albums to his credit—and a career that was based on nostalgia, not just for the music of another era but for the memory of his brother—Jimmie wasn't exactly where he wanted to be in life. The problem wasn't so much getting there as envisioning exactly where that place should be.

It seemed like only yesterday that he was a teenager, filled with the newly discovered, gut-burning fire of blues and rock 'n' roll. What a pleasure it had been to spend his evenings in smoke-filled nightclubs, playing the music that he loved. Now he was approaching fifty, and the world looked radically different.

It was still fun to play his guitar, but his expectations were different now, lowered by more than thirty hard years on the road. He had to face the sobering reality that any music he made in the future would not go anywhere it had not already been in the past. He could refine it, of course—add innovative bells and whistles—but he knew that spectrum was not unlimited.

Jimmie took a close look at his life. Although he had made it through the drug and alcohol years intact, his marriage had not. He and Connie had made it through their teenage years together, all the wild and crazy years on the road, even through Stevie's death, but they couldn't make it through the quiet years that followed. They divorced quietly, without public rancor, and moved on with their separate lives.

"She was there by Jimmie's side through a whole lot of shit," said Preston Hubbard. "I lost contact with her . . . she's very reclusive now. She hasn't stayed in contact. Lou Ann [Barton] was one of her best friends and she rarely sees her. She just moved on."

Jimmie moved on too, but in a slightly different way. He continued to work on his relationship with his mother, and he added a son to his family—Tyrone Vaughan, the son by Becky Crabtree he had vociferously rejected as his flesh and blood. After nearly thirty years, Jimmie had a change of heart, for reasons known only to him, and publicly embraced Tyrone as his son. Jimmie had the look of a man who wanted to put his life in order.

Another change he made was to part company with his manager Mark Proct, who had been with him for most of his career, and put his career in the hands of Cory L. Moore, whose first priority was to get his client a new record deal. He turned to Artemis Records, a small New York–based label that successfully marketed retro artists who had fallen out of favor after long careers.

Before starting work on his third solo album—*Do You Get the Blues?*—Jimmie immersed himself in the music of his youth, especially Sarah Vaughan, Thelonious Monk, and Gene Ammons. He had every intention of recording another blues album, but he wanted it to have some of the romantic jazz influences that he had enjoyed as a teen and young adult.

"When you're listening to Thelonious Monk or Mile Davis's 'Kind of Blue.' It's romantic," Jimmie explained to the *Asbury Park Press*. "Or it seems romantic to me, anyway. It evokes all these feelings when you hear it, and I wanted to do something that gave you that feeling and had dirty blues guitar on it at the same time. . . . [It is] romantic in a way that a lot of the old Blue Note records are romantic. I think we can all use a little more romance. Anytime."

This time around, Jimmie decided to produce the album himself. Asked by Guitar.com why he wanted to do that, he attributed his decision to the smaller budgets that independent labels offer and the fact that he sometimes found himself disagreeing with Nile Rodgers and John Hampton over how his albums should be recorded. Instead, he hired Hampton to be the engineer (a smaller expense). Even so, as in past recordings, the basic tracks for most of the album were recorded at Ardent Studios in Memphis.

"Dirty Girl," the leadoff song on the album, is a gritty Memphis-style instrumental written by Bill Willis, the organ player. With Jimmie on guitar, Willis on organ, and George Rains on drums, it was the sort of jukebox song that would have been a major hit in the late 1950s or early 1960s.

For "The Deep End," Jimmie plays slide guitar and boogies alongside James Cotton, one of the best harmonica players around. The B3 was used just enough to be effective and not a bit more. Jimmie seems at ease with the vocal, primarily because it was recorded in a key that allows him maximum creativity for his limited range.

"Without You" was written by Jimmie's son, Tyrone, who also played rhythm guitar on the track. "My son wrote the lyrics and the music . . . with this friend of his, and I just did the song my way," Jimmie told the *Asbury Park Sunday Press*. "I sort of changed it up to suit me. I usually do that anyway with whatever song."

One of the best songs on the album is "Don't Let the Sun Set," cowritten by Jimmie. It challenged Jimmie vocally, primarily because of the nuances the song required him to display to flow in and out of the changes, but Jimmie rose to the occasion and nailed it with confidence. The song begins oddly with Jimmie playing in unison with flutist Herman Green, a veteran Memphis sax and flute player.

Jimmie later jokingly told reporters that he added the flute to "piss off the blues nerds." More to the point, he told the *Tennessean* that he wanted to add a sense of humor to his music and he thought that a flute would be the perfect vehicle.

"It's my own kind of art and I feel personal with it," Jimmie explained. "I'm expressing myself and playing the kind of music I want to hear, because I can't hear it anywhere else. So I have to make it."

For the tracks recorded in Texas, Lou Ann Barton joined Jimmie on "Power of Love" and "In the Middle of the Night," which also featured Tommy Shannon and Chris Layton. Besides the flute, the album was different because most of the songs were recorded without an electric bass. Instead, Bill Willis played bass with his left hand on the keyboard, giving the songs a lusher bottom.

One other thing that set *Do You Get the Blues?* apart from his previous solo efforts was that Jimmie finally learned how to write an ending to his songs. That new skill was taken to the extreme on "Planet Bongo," an instrumental that include a flute and a soulful chorus. It is one of the most sophisticated songs he has ever written, not harmed in the least by one of the most elaborate endings in song-writing history.

Do You Get the Blues? is a far cry from the albums Jimmie recorded with the T-Birds or the album he did with Stevie, but it showed real growth, a splendid thing for a man who turned fifty the year of its release.

"There's so much weird stuff going on in music now, I just wanted to boil the pot down and get dirty," he told the *Albany Herald*. "It was all a matter of doing what I felt at the time. Oddly, this is the rawest, bluesiest album I've done, but there are soul and pop tunes on there, too. It all seemed to fit."

As they had done on his two previous solo projects, Jimmie and John Hampton took the analog tape they had recorded at Ardent to Jimmie's home in Austin, where they worked on the tape using a Pro Tool, a computerized software system that enables its user to edit tapes in a variety of ways. Off-key notes, from a musical instrument or human vocal cords, can be made pitch perfect with the twist of a knob.

"If a singer sings a flat note, you find the note, push a button, and it is in pitch," said Hampton. "If you find a guitar lick that is five milliseconds late, you edit it and scoot it to where it is right dead on the beat."

Unlike the early days with the T-Birds, when they went into a studio, recorded the songs, and left the mixing to an engineer, Jimmie felt a need to fine-tune his music. It was what everyone else was doing, so why shouldn't he?

"I just moved in with him—he's got a spare bedroom," said Hampton. "We roll a Pro Tool in there and work on the tape at his house. He has a great-sounding living room. You can cut guitars there, and he's got an organ."

Unfortunately, after going over every song, time and time again, Jimmie and Hampton were unable to agree on the finished product. "We kind of lost it," said Hampton. "It was probably my fault because I was anti–Pro Tool and he found someone in Austin who would work for next to nothing, and who would play the Pro Tool game with him and I kind of bowed out of it." Hampton returned to Memphis, where he ended up becoming more of a fan of the Pro Tool computer system.

When *Do You Get the Blues?* was released in October 2001, it was greeted with mixed reviews. The *Boston Herald* found the album "tasteful," but complained that the vocals were "not just weak of tone, they're also tame and inexpressive." Countering that opinion was a critic from the *Lexington Herald-Leader*, who found the album the "work of a guitar stylist speaking profoundly as he dodges the obvious. His groove remains fun, flexible and, above all, original." *Pulse* magazine noted that while Jimmie had not "achieved the deity status of his younger brother, Stevie Ray (death is a prerequisite for sainthood) some believe the understated, 'atmospheric' blues he's recorded since leaving the Fabulous Thunderbirds makes him the more interesting of the pair."

Jimmie told interviewers that he didn't consider his music to be a relic of the past. "I didn't go and evaluate the market before I made this record," he told the *North Bay Bohemian*. "I mean, I think my records are current. They're not nostalgia records. They've got a lot of roots in them, and it is blues and this and it's got all kinds of elements in it. . . . I'm not trying to make an authentic, looking-back kind of record. To me this [music] is like now."

To promote the album, Jimmie put together a touring band made up of people who had worked with him in the studio—Lou Ann Barton, Bill Willis, George Rains, Billy Pittman, Greg Sain, and Charlie Redd—and hit the road. At the Los Angeles House of Blues, he performed before a crowd of about one thousand, giving a performance that *Variety* described as "delivering the goods, Texas style."

In a review of a February 2002 performance in St. Petersburg, Florida, the *St. Petersburg Times* declared in the headline of its review that "Vaughan Has All the Right Answers." After providing a breakdown of his musical experience, the critic wrote "that musical seasoning was evident . . . when he brought his lean, clean, six-string lines, Texas rhythms, slicked-back hair and vintage threads."

A couple of weeks later, Jimmie flew to Los Angeles, where he attended the forty-fourth annual Grammy Awards. To his delight, he won a Grammy for Best Traditional Blues Album for *Do You Get the Blues?* It was his fourth win, the other three coming from his collaboration with Stevie on *Family Style* and for his involvement with the

1996 *Shuffle: A Tribute to Stevie Ray Vaughan*, but it was his first win for a record that did not involve his brother.

Jimmie toured for most of 2002, discovering the awful truth that while his music was still popular in small venues, where the faithful gathered to drink and share memories of better days, that popularity did not translate into record sales. He ended up severing his relationship with Artemis Records after one album and returned to Austin, where he focused again on his vintage cars.

In January 2003, he went to New York to participate in a star-studded Salute to the Blues concert at Radio City Music Hall. For blues fans, it was an exciting event, for along with Jimmie Vaughan were Solomon Burke, Natalie Cole, B. B. King, Dr. John, Clarence "Gatemouth" Brown, John Fogerty, Buddy Guy, Robert Cray, Bonnie Raitt, and dozens of others. It was meant to kick off a year-long celebration of the blues, compliments of the United States Congress, which had declared 2003 the Year of the Blues.

The one thing that all the great blues musicians and recording artists shared, in addition to a lifelong love of the music, was the disquieting fact that, despite the rich history they shared, none of them had had hit records in years, if ever. That is the sad reality of the blues, and it may be one reason why Jimmie became so reclusive in his later years and so inexplicably hostile to the music press.

Stevie Ray Vaughan is better liked by the music press because he offered more flash and fire, took more chances musically than his brother, and always found time to talk to music writers about his latest project. In some respects, Jimmie is just the opposite. In his mind, flash belongs in a souped-up hot rod or in the clothes he wears when he's performing, not in his music; he doesn't take chances because he likes to paint within the lines; and he doesn't feel comfortable talking to music writers, mainly because they always seem to want to talk about things he doesn't think are important.

"I try to speak with my guitar in sentences," Jimmie once said. "The people that I enjoy and the music that I enjoy are not about just a bunch of licks strung together. If you just play a bunch of guitar licks that aren't connected, it's like throwing a lot of words into a bowl. It doesn't make any sense. It's just words."

Jimmie has more records inside him, but whether he will allow them to emerge or not is questionable. Why record another blues album when sales are predetermined by an audience that gets smaller with each passing year? Jimmie and Stevie made their mark on American music when they were young and indefatigable. With nothing else to prove, no new ground to break, why try to justify old victories?

Playing the "joints," as Kim Wilson likes to call them, doesn't have the same appeal that it had when Jimmie was in his teens and twenties, when young women literally stood in line to bestow favors on him. He doesn't need the money now, thanks to Stevie's continuing success, and the hot-blooded adulation of women in their sixties and seventies hardly seems worth the mind-numbing late hours required to receive it.

Jimmie is at a good place in his life. He may just want to stay there.

The Fabulous Thunderbirds: (l–r) Jimmie Vaughan, Mike Buck, Kim Wilson, Keith Ferguson. Photo: PhotoFest

The Fabulous Thunderbirds: (l–r) Fran Christina, Jimmie Vaughan, Keith Ferguson, Kim Wilson. Photo: PhotoFest

The Fabulous Thunderbirds: (l–r) Preston Hubbard, Jimmie Vaughan, Fran Christina, Kim Wilson. Photo: PhotoFest

Jimmie Vaughan, left, Kim Wilson on *Austin City Limits*. Photo by Scott Newton (PhotoFest)

Jimmie Vaughan at the Memphis fairgrounds in 1986. Photo by James L. Dickerson

Kim Wilson at the Memphis fairgrounds. Photo by James L. Dickerson

Jimmie Vaughan plays his battered Fender. Photo by James L. Dickerson

Kim Wilson, Jimmie Vaughan, Dave Edmunds at Ardent Studios in Memphis. Photo by James L. Dickerson

Dave Edmunds and Kim Wilson lose it at Memphis's Ardent Studios. Photo by James L. Dickerson

David Porter in the 1960s, while writing hit songs for Stax Records. Photo: Mississippi Valley Collection, University of Memphis, University Libraries

Kim Wilson, Jimmie Vaughan, Dave Edmunds at Ardent Studios. Photo by James L. Dickerson

The Memphis Horns, Andrew Love, left, and Wayne Jackson, in a Memphis studio. Photo by Greg Campbell

Stevie Ray Vaughan at a Memphis hotel. Photo by James L. Dickerson

Chris Layton during sound check at Memphis's Mud Island. Photo by James L. Dickerson

Stevie Ray Vaughan in Memphis. Photo by James L. Dickerson

Stevie Ray Vaughan. Photo by James L. Dickerson

Stevie Ray Vaughan and Double Trouble on Mud Island. Photo by James L. Dickerson

Stevie Ray Vaughan in Memphis.
Photo by James L. Dickerson

Stevie Ray Vaughan in Memphis.
Photo by James L. Dickerson

Stevie Ray Vaughan consults with Reese Wynans during sound check. Photo by James L. Dickerson

Brown Burnett, left, and Stevie Ray Vaughan during an interview. Photo by James L. Dickerson

Jimmie Vaughan in publicity photo for *Do You Get the Blues?* Photo by James Minchin III

Discography

Jimmie Vaughn and Stevie Ray Vaughan

Family Style (1990)
    Epic-Sony Records
    Producer: Nile Rodgers
    Engineer: John Hampton
    "Hard to Be"
    "White Boots"
    "D/FW"
    "Good Texan"
    "Hillbillies from Outerspace"
    "Long Way from Home"
    "Tick Tock"
    "Telephone Song"
    "Baboom/Mama Said"
    "Brothers"

Stevie Ray Vaughan

SRV [Box Set] (2000)
    Sony Records
    Producers: Various

Engineers: Various
Disc 1:
  "Thunderbird"
  "I'm Cryin'"
  "You're Gonna Miss Me Baby"
  "They Call Me Guitar Hurricane"
  "All Your Love"
  "Come on (Part I)
  "Letter to My Girlfriend"
  "Lenny"
  "Don't Lose Your Cool"
  "Crosscut Saw"
  "Manic Depression"
  "Texas Flood"
  "Collins' Shuffle"
  "Pride and Joy"
  "Love Struck Baby"
  "Hug You, Squeeze You"
  "Don't Stop by the Creek, Son"
  "Ask Me No Questions"
Disc 2:
  "Scuttle Buttin'"
  "Couldn't Stand the Weather"
  "Empty Arms"
  "Little Wing/Third Stone from the Sun"
  "If You Have to Know"
  "These Blues Is Killing Me"
  "Boilermaker"
  "Change It"
  "Shake 'N Bake"
  "Mary Had a Little Lamb"
  "I'm Leaving You"
  "Rude Mood/Pipeline"
  "Sky Is Crying"
  "Voodoo Chile"
Disc 3:
  "Lookin' Out the Window"
  "Look at Little Sister"

"Willie the Wimp"
"House Is Rockin'"
"Crossfire"
"Wall of Denial"
"Dirty Pool"
"Going Down"
"Rude Mood"
"Pride and Joy"
"Testify"
"Long Way from Home"
"Tightrope"
"Cold Shot"
"Things That I Used to Do"
"Let Me Love You Baby"
"Leave My Girl Alone"

Live at Carnegie Hall (1997)
Sony Records
Producer: Stevie Ray Vaughan
Engineer: Unknown
"Intro: John Hammond Jr."
"Scuttle Buttin'"
"Love Struck Baby"
"Honey Bee"
"Cold Shot"
"Letter to My Girlfriend"
"Dirty Pool"
"Pride and Joy"
"Things That I Used to Do"
"C.O.D."
"Iced Over"
"Lenny"
"Rude Mood"

In the Beginning (1992)
Epic-Sony Records
Producer: Stevie Ray Vaughan
Engineer: Malcolm Harper and Wayne Bell

"In the Open"
"Slide Thing"
"They Call Me Guitar Hurricane"
"All Your Love"
"I Miss Loving"
"Tin Pan Alley"
"Love Struck Baby"
"Tell Me"
"Shake for Me"
"Live Another Day"

The Sky Is Crying (1991)
Epic Records
Producers: Jim Gaines and others
Engineers: Various
"Boot Hill"
"The Sky Is Crying"
"Empty Arms"
"Little Wing"
"Wham!"
"May I Have a Talk with You"
"Close to You"
"Chitlins Con Carne"
"So Excited"
"Life by the Drop"

In Step (1989)
Epic Records
Producer: Jim Gaines
Engineer: Jim Gaines
"The House Is Rockin'"
"Crossfire"
"Tightrope"
"Let Me Love You Baby"
"Leave My Girl Alone"
"Travis Walk"
"Wall of Denial"

"Scratch-N-Sniff"
"Love Me Darlin'"
"Riviera Paradise"

Live Alive! (1986)
Epic Records
Producer: Stevie Ray Vaughan
Engineer: Various
"Say What"
"Ain't Gone 'n' Give Up on Love"
"Pride and Joy"
"Mary Had a Little Lamb"
"Superstition"
"I'm Leaving You"
"Cold Shot"
"Willie the Wimp"
"Look at Little Sister"
"Texas Flood"
"Voodoo Chile"
"Love Struck Baby"
"Change It"

Soul to Soul (1985)
Epic Records
Producers: Stevie Ray Vaughan, Double Trouble, Richard
      Mullen
Engineer: Richard Mullen
"Say What!"
"Lookin' Out the Window"
"Look at Little Sister"
"Ain't Gone 'n' Give Up on Love"
"Gone Home"
"Change It"
"You'll Be Mine"
"Empty Arms"
"Come on (Part III)"
"Life without You"

Couldn't Stand the Weather (1985)
> Epic Records
> Producers: Stevie Ray Vaughan, Chris Layton, Tommy Shannon, Richard Mullen, Jim Capfer
> Engineers: Richard Mullen
> "Scuttle Buttin'"
> "Couldn't Stand the Weather"
> "The Things (That) I Used to Do"
> "Voodoo Chile (Slight Return)"
> "Cold Shot"
> "Tin Pan Alley"
> "Honey Bee"
> "Stang's Swang"

Texas Flood (1983)
> Epic Records
> Producer: Stevie Ray Vaughan
> Engineer: Richard Mullen
> "Love Struck Baby"
> "Pride and Joy"
> "Texas Flood"
> "Tell Me"
> "Testify"
> "Rude Mood"
> "Mary Had a Little Lamb"
> "Dirty Pool"
> "I'm Cryin'"
> "Lenny"

Jimmie Vaughan

Do You Get the Blues? (2001)
> Artemis Records
> Producer: Jimmie Vaughan
> Engineer: John Hampton, Jared Tuten
> "Dirty Girl"
> "Out of the Shadows"

"The Deep End"
"Power of Love"
"Without You"
"Let Me In"
"Don't Let the Sun Set"
"Robbin' Me Blind"
"Slow Dance Blues"
"In the Middle of the Night"
"Planet Bongo"

Out There (1998)
    Epic Records
    Producer: Jimmie Vaughan, John Hampton, Nile Rodgers
    Engineer: John Hampton
    "Like a King"
    "Lost in You"
    "Out There"
    "Can't Say No"
    "The Ironic Twist"
    "Positively Meant to Be"
    "Motor Head Baby"
    "Kinky Woman"
    "Astral Projection Blues"
    "Little Son, Big Sun"

Strange Pleasure (1994)
    Epic Records
    Producers: Jimmie Vaughan, Nile Rodgers
    Engineer: Gary Tole, John Hampton
    "Boom-Bapa-Boom"
    "Don't Cha Know"
    "Hey-Yeah"
    "Flamenco Dancer"
    "Everybody's Got Sweet Soul Vibe"
    "Tilt A Whirl"
    "Six Strings Down"
    "Just Like Putty"

"Two Wings"
"Love the World"
"Strange Pleasure"

Wrap It Up (with the Fabulous Thunderbirds) (1993)
Sony Music
Producers: Various
Engineers: Various
"Wrap It Up"
"It Takes a Big Man to Cry"
"Stagger Lee"
"Now Loosen Up Baby"
"Feelin' Good"
"Tuff Enuff"
"Knock Yourself Out"
"Twist It Off"
"It Comes to Me Naturally"
"Born to Love You"

Powerful Stuff (with the Fabulous Thunderbirds) (1989)
CBS
Producer: Terry Manning
Engineer: Terry Manning
"Rock This Place"
"Knock Yourself Out"
"Mistake Number 1"
"One Night Stand"
"Emergency"
"Powerful Stuff"
"Close Together"
"Now Loosen Up Baby"
"She's Hot"
"Rainin' in My Heart"

Hot Number (with the Fabulous Thunderbirds) (1987)
CBS
Producer: Dave Edmunds

Engineer: Dave Charles
"Stand Back"
"Hot Number"
"Wasted Tears"
"It Comes to Me Naturally"
"Love in Common"
"How Do You Spell Love"
"Streets of Gold"
"Sofa Circuit"
"Don't Bother Tryin' to Steal Her Love"
"It Takes a Big Man to Cry"

Tuff Enuff (with the Fabulous Thunderbirds) (1986)
CBS Records
Producer: Dave Edmunds
Engineer: Carey Taylor
"Tuff Enuff"
"Tell Me"
"Look at That, Look at That"
"Two Times My Lovin'"
"Amnesia"
"Wrap It Up"
"True Love"
"Why Get Up"
"I Don't Care"
"Down at Antones"

T-Bird Rhythm (with the Fabulous Thunderbirds) (1982)
Chrysalis Records
Producer: Nick Lowe
Engineer: Colin Fairley
"Can't Tear It Up Enuff"
"How Do You Spell Love"
"You're Humbuggin' Me"
"My Babe"
"Neighbor Tend to Your Business"
"The Monkey"

"Diddy with Daddy"
"Lover's Crime"
"Poor Boy"
"Tell Me (Pretty Baby)"
"Gotta Have Some/Just Got Home"

Butt Rockin' (with the Fabulous Thunderbirds) (1981)
   Chrysalis Records
   Producer: Denny Bruce
   Engineer: Kim King, Tom Gandalf
   "I Believe I'm in Love"
   "One's Too Many"
   "Give Me All Your Lovin'"
   "Roll, Roll, Roll"
   "Cherry Pink and Apple Blossom White"
   "I Hear You Knocking"
   "Tip On In"
   "I'm Sorry"
   "Mathilda"
   "Tell Me Why"
   "In Orbit"
   "Found a New Love"
   Bonus tracks on Benchmark Records reissue:
   "I Got Eyes"
   "Someday You'll Want Me"

What's the Word? (with the Fabulous Thunderbirds) (1980)
   Chrysalis Records
   Producer: Denny Bruce
   Engineer: Bob Sullivan
   "Runnin' Shows"
   "You Ain't Nothing but Fine"
   "Low-Down Woman"
   "Extra Jimmies"
   "Sugar Coated Love"
   "Last Call for Alcohol"
   "The Crawl"

"Jumpin' Bad"
"Learn to Treat Me Right"
"I'm a Good Man (If You Give Me a Chance)"
"Dirty Work"
"That's Enough of That Stuff"
Bonus tracks on Benchmark Records reissue:
"Band Introduction by C-Boy"
"Bad Boy"
"Scratch My Back"
"Los Fabulosos Thunderbirds"

The Fabulous Thunderbirds (Girls Go Wild) (1979)
Chrysalis Records
Producer: Denny Bruce
Engineer: Bob Sullivan
"Wait On Time"
"Scratch My Back"
"Rich Woman"
"Full-Time Lover"
"Pocket Rocket"
"She's Tuff"
"Marked Deck"
"Walkin' to My Baby"
"Rock with Me"
"C-Boy's Blues"
"Let Me In"

Bibliography

Interviews by Author

Stevie Ray Vaughan
Jimmie Vaughan
Kim Wilson
Preston Hubbard
Fran Christina
B. B. King
Dave Edmunds
Jim Gaines
John Hampton
Jerry Lee Lewis
John Fry
Ron Wood
Robert Pittman
Gregg Geller
Bobby Manuel
Estelle Axton
Carla Thomas
Chips Moman

Charles Comer
Ringo Starr
Carl Perkins
Brown Burnett
Don Nix
Jimmy Davis
Robert Cray
Dick Hackett
Al Green
Bobby Womack

Books

Booth, Stanley. *Rhythm Oil: A Journey through the Music of the American South*. New York: Pantheon, 1991.
Dickerson, James L. *Coming Home: 21 Conversations about Memphis Music*. Memphis: Scripps Howard, 1985.
———. *Goin' Back to Memphis: A Century of Blues, Rock 'n' Roll, and Glorious Soul*. New York: Schirmer, 1996.
Goldrosen, John, and John Beecher. *The Definitive Biography of Buddy Holly*. New York: Penguin, 1975.
Handy, W. C. *Father of the Blues: An Autobiography*. New York: DaCapo, 1941.
Harkins, John E. *Metropolis of the American Nile*. Oxford, Miss.: Guild Bindery, 1991.
Herzhaft, Gerard. *Encyclopedia of the Blues*. Fayetteville: University of Arkansas Press, 1992.
Kitts, Jeff, Brad Tolinski, and Harold Steinblatt, eds. *Stevie Ray Vaughan: In His Own Words*. Milwaukee, Wis.: Hal Leonard, 1997.
Leigh, Keri. *Stevie Ray: Soul to Soul*. Dallas: Taylor, 1993.
MvAleer, Dave. *The All Music Book of Hit Singles from 1954 to the Present Day*. London: Carlton, 1994.
Palmer, Robert. *Deep Blues*. New York: Penguin, 1982.
Patoski, Joe Nick, and Bill Crawford. *Stevie Ray Vaughan: Caught in the Crossfire*. Boston: Little, Brown, 1993.
Thompson, Dave. *Winona Ryder*. Dallas: Taylor, 1996.

Magazines and Newspapers

Backett, Matt. "Trigger Fingers." *Guitar Player*, February 2002.

Baldwin, Dawn. "Inside the U2/Sun Studio Sessions." *Memphis Star*, December 1987.

Bessette, Katherine. "The Jeff Beck Interview." *Outer Shell*, n.d.

Bialczak, Mark. "Lineup Announced for R&B Festival in Syracuse." *Syracuse Post-Standard*, April 16, 2002.

Birnbaum, Larry. "Born Near the Bayou." *Guitar World*, September 1986.

————. "The Fabulous Thunderbirds." *Down Beat*, February 1986.

Booth, Philip. "Vaughan Has All the Right Answers." *St. Petersburg Times*, February 19, 2002.

Burnett, Brown. "Otis Redding: Stax Records Survivors on 20th Anniversary of Soulmate's Death." *Nine-O-One Network*, February 1988.

————. "Singer Brings Her Blues Home." *Commercial Appeal*, September 14, 1984.

————. "Spirit of Blues Triumphs to Cap Awards Program." *Commercial Appeal*, November 17, 1983.

————. "Wearing the Label." *Nine-O-One Network*, October 1987.

Cartwright, Ryan. "The Other Blues Brother." *Nashville Tennessean*, February 8, 2002.

Cote, Michael. "Jimmie Vaughan." *Blues Revue*, December-January 2002.

Crawford, Bill. "The Artistic Afterlife." *Austin Chronicle* 15, no. 6.

Dickerson, James. "B. B. King." *Nine-O-One Network*, December 1987.

————. "The Fabulous Thunderbirds Get a Memphis Groove." *Nine-O-One Network*, May-June 1987.

————. "Fabulous Thunderbirds: Texas Band Toughs It Out to the Top." *Nine-O-One Network*, September-October 1986.

————. "Handys Flow in Memorable Night for the Blues." *Commercial Appeal*, November 18, 1985.

————. "Interview with Gregg Geller." *Nine-O-One Network*, March-April 1987.

————. "Interview with Robert Pittman." *Nine-O-One Network*, July-August 1987.

———. "Interview with Ron Wood." *Nine-O-One Network*, September-October 1986.

———. "Memphis Is Getting Groovier." *Commercial Appeal*, March 1, 1986.

———. "Memphis Misses the Hits." *Commercial Appeal*, 1991.

———. "Together Again." *Nine-O-One Network*, November-December 1986.

Donahue, Michael. "'Handys' on Tap in Blues Salute." *Commercial Appeal*, November 15, 1986.

Drozdowski, Ted. "Guitar Slingers Shoot It Out." *Rolling Stone*, November 10, 1989.

———. "Jimmie Vaughan." *Pulse*, November 2001.

———. "Sex and Strings." *Boston Phoenix*, October 23, 2001.

Ebert, Roger. "Cocktail." *Chicago Sun-Times*, July 29, 1988.

Ferguson, Dan. "Jimmie Vaughan's Guitar Work Is All about Finesse and Soul." *Standard Times* (North Kingstown, R.I.), October 25, 2001.

Ferman, Dave. "Ten Years Later, No One Holds a Candle to Stevie Ray Vaughan." *New York Times*, September 3, 2000.

Fletcher, Carlton. "Family Tradition." *Albany Herald*, February 8, 2002.

Friedman, Josh Alan. "Beautiful Loser." *Dallas Observer*, March 28, 1996.

Gates, David, and Devin Gordon. "Smooth as Santana." *Newsweek*, February 14, 2000.

Gewertz, Daniel. "Tanvas, Yonder Mountain Add New Life to Old Styles." *Boston Herald*, October 26, 2001.

Gill, Chris. "Nile Rodgers: '70s Groove with a '90s Attitude." *Guitar Player*, June 1992.

Gilmore, Mikal. "Blues Summit: The Fateful Weekend." *Rolling Stone*, October 4, 1990.

Holdship, Bill. "Jimmie Vaughan Concert Review." *Variety*, November 16, 2001.

Jolson-Colburn, Jeffrey. "House of Blues Moves into Red Hot Multimedia Mode." *Hollywood Reporter*, April 18, 1996.

Maese, Rick A. "Jimmie Vaughan." *Albuquerque Tribune*, November 23, 2001.

Moser, Margaret. "All-American." *Austin Chronicle*, November 23, 2001.

———. "Blood and Memories." *Austin Chronicle* 18, no. 32.

Oshea, Jamie. "Jimmie Lee Vaughan's Kandy-Green Kustom Kaddy." *Juxtapoz*, n.d.

Padgett. "Guitar Family Feud." *Orlando Weekly*, February 14, 2002.

Paul, Alan. "Blues Brother." *Guitar World*, December 2001.

Rodgers, Larry. "Jimmie Gets the Blues, Do You?" *Arizona Republic*, November 15, 2001.

Sculley, Alan. "Back on Track." *North Bay Bohemian*, November 8, 2001.

———. "Vaughan Looks for New Sound with 'Blues' Tour." *North County Times*, November 1, 2001.

Seigal, Buddy. "O, Brother, Where's Thou Art?" *OC Weekly*, November 9, 2001.

Shuster, Fred. "Blues Boy." *Los Angeles Daily News*, November 8, 2001.

Sinclair, Tom. "Stevie Ray's Last Flight." *Newsweek*, September 1, 2000.

Skelly, Richard. "Romancing the Blues." *Asbury Park Press*, October 22, 2001.

Steinberg, David. "Duke City Is Getting the Blues with Jimmie Vaughan." *Albuquerque Journal*, November 16, 2001.

Sutcliffe, Phil. "Jimmie Vaughan." *Blender*, November 2001.

Tipaldi, Art. "Tommy Shannon." *Dallas Observer*, December 25, 1997.

Tunis, Walter. "Jimmie Vaughan." *Lexington Herald-Leader*, September 14, 2001.

Walsh, Christopher. "Ardent Still Molds Sounds of Memphis." *Billboard*, February 2, 2002.

Weiss, Arlene. "Jimmie Vaughan Storms 'ACL.'" *Vintage Guitar*, January 2002.

Wynn, Ron. "Songs of Greeting to Moman Are Grumbles Three Years Later." *Commercial Appeal*, April 30, 1989.

Zonkel, Phillip. "Blues Unplugged." *Press-Telegram* (Long Beach, Calif.), April 4, 2002.

Index